W9-BLP-691

Please remember that this is a library book,
and that it belongs only temporarily to each
person who uses it. Be considerate. Do
not write in this, or any, library book.

The Learning Connection

NEW PARTNERSHIPS BETWEEN SCHOOLS AND COLLEGES

Gene I. Maeroff
Patrick M. Callan
Michael D. Usdan

EDITORS

Teachers College, Columbia University
New York and London

Published by Teachers College Press, 1234 Amsterdam Avenue, New York, NY 10027

Library of Congress Cataloging-in-Publication Data

The learning connection : new partnerships between schools and colleges / Gene I.
  Maeroff, Patrick M. Callan, Michael D. Usdan, editors.
    p. cm.
  ISBN 0-8077-4017-9 (pbk.)
    1. College-school cooperation—United States—Case studies. I. Maeroff, Gene I.
II. Callan, Patrick M.   III. Usdan, Michael D.
LB2331.53 .L395 2001
378.1'03—dc21   00-062899

ISBN 0-8077-4017-9 (paper)

Printed on acid-free paper

Manufactured in the United States of America
08 07 06 05 04 03 02 01   8 7 6 5 4 3 2 1

CONTENTS

FOREWORD

The chasm between schools and colleges is an indication of dysfunction, a phenomenon that is increasingly recognized as a major impediment to the successful education of all students. High standards and improved schools and colleges will, we strongly suggest, ultimately depend on the extent to which this gap can be narrowed.

The Learning Connection: New Partnerships Between Schools and Colleges describes 12 programs that are now attempting to overcome the disadvantages of this separation. These case studies are organized around five themes—governance, equity, standards, teacher preparation, and community building. All of these programs, however, share a fundamental purpose—collaboration on behalf of improved student learning.

The documentation of these programs is timely. The rhetoric of "K–16" is becoming more common, but collaboration intended to improve learning still remains an area that falls far short of its potential. The successes and failures of these programs offer valuable insights about the rewards and pitfalls of collaboration. Both practitioners and policy makers can profit from the experiences described in this book.

We are pleased that the Hechinger Institute on Education and the Media, the Institute for Educational Leadership, and the National Center for Public Policy and Higher Education have joined to sponsor this publication. We are grateful for the financial support of the Ewing Marion Kauffman Foundation that made the project and this volume possible.

James B. Hunt, Jr.
Governor, North Carolina
Chairman, National Center for
Public Policy and Higher Education

Arthur Levine
President
Teachers College
Columbia University

James J. Renier
Retired Chairman
Honeywell Corporation
Chairman, Board of Directors,
The Institute for Educational Leadership

Acknowledgments

This volume reflects the work and commitment of many individuals and several organizations. The editors would like to thank, above all, the Ewing Marion Kauffman Foundation for its generous support, without which this project would not have been possible.

Thanks go, too, to the journalists who did the field studies and wrote the individual chapters. Their snapshot portrayals of 12 diverse interlevel initiatives will provide, for the first decade of the new century, important findings and benchmarks for the more detailed and research-oriented analyses that we expect will gain the attention of scholars. We expect that educators and policy makers will also make use of these portrayals as they look for new ways to bind precollegiate and higher education.

The editors would also like to express appreciation for the support and contributions of their colleagues at each of the participating organizations—the Hechinger Institute on Education and the Media, the National Center for Public Policy and Higher Education, and the Institute for Educational Leadership.

Gene I. Maeroff, New York
Patrick M. Callan, San Jose
Michael D. Usdan, Washington D.C.

The Learning Connection

NEW PARTNERSHIPS BETWEEN SCHOOLS AND COLLEGES

A Relationship Waiting to Happen

The long-neglected relationship between elementary–secondary (K–12) and postsecondary education is beginning to receive some of the attention it merits. Visible bits and pieces of interlevel programs are emerging throughout the country. With the exception of the relatively new Education Trust, the College Board, the Southern Regional Education Board, and a few other entities, however, only a handful of significant organizations and networks are explicitly designed to link the educational sectors in meaningful ways. In the main, efforts to promote interlevel relationships have consisted of underfunded, ephemeral initiatives that have been episodic and nonsystemic in nature. Despite recent positive developments in such states as Georgia, Maryland, and Oregon and in some individual communities, interlevel collaboration remains largely invisible and unexplored. The two educational levels are still, for the most part, self-contained universes that exist in "splendid isolation" from each other.[1]

In other words, there is in most places a profound disjuncture and continuing cultural, political, and institutional chasm between K–12 and higher education. The two sectors live apart—having separate associations, professional worlds, and networks—instead of existing as a coherent community of leaders. What Roland Barth of the Harvard Graduate School of Education would call "dual citizenship" remains evanescent. The two sectors—at a time when both need reform, renewal, rethinking, and restructuring—have few connecting mechanisms to enable them to work cooperatively on issues of mutual concern. The issues that could link the sectors are of growing importance but remain on the margin, under nobody's responsibility. Thus, there is no direct constituency; interface issues remain largely submerged. Neither sector welcomes the other onto its turf. The "impossible dream" of partnership between schools and colleges remains as elusive as that pursued by the Man of La Mancha.

This report is predicated on the contention that more intensive efforts are needed to place interlevel relationships on the nation's educational policy agenda. These efforts, if embraced, have the potential to change the structure and operation of both sides of the educational equation in significant ways. In all likelihood, however, significant external forces will be required to prod and drive the necessary discussion and debate; educators do not seem ready to make these moves on their own.

So much is at stake that leverage might have to come from the intervention of the influential business and political leaders who have been so instrumental in forcing and sustaining K–12 education reform in recent years. There is little recognition in the professional education world, much less in the lay community, that only the United States has such a degree of K–16 separation. The general public as well as most policy analysts are seemingly oblivious to the fact that there still are too few attempts to bridge the chasm that separates the two sectors. There is certainly insufficient research and study of the problem.

The dozen case studies in this volume were written by a diverse group of journalists under the auspices of the Hechinger Institute on Education and the Media at Teachers College, Columbia University, for the explicit purpose of exploring and documenting the current status of interlevel issues. The reporters followed a common protocol (see Appendix), which focused on questions or conditions that either deter or facilitate school and college cooperation and collaboration. This publication, we believe, serves as a unique, seminal resource for policy makers and practitioners at all educational levels. We hope it will be particularly useful as the saliency of interlevel issues escalates dramatically in the years immediately ahead, as we expect will happen.

These case studies were supported through the generosity of a grant from the Ewing Marion Kauffman Foundation. The report represents a joint initiative by three nonprofit organizations—the Hechinger Institute, the Institute for Educational Leadership in Washington, D.C., and the National Center for Public Policy and Higher Education in San Jose, California. These organizations have unique and complementary strengths and specialized outreach to diverse and important audiences. The Hechinger Institute works on education policy issues with the nation's journalists. The Institute for Educational Leadership has long-established networks of programs and contacts with public school policy makers in communities throughout the country and at every governmental level. The National Center for Public Policy and Higher Education is an independent organization that stimulates the creation of public policies to improve opportunity and achievement in higher education.

This volume, then, assumes that the time is propitious to pull together and analyze in a single publication growing numbers of fragmented initiatives that are making interlevel relationships a more visible policy issue. The 12 case studies of interlevel cooperation described here have enjoyed varying degrees of success. That the document is written by journalists, in our estimation, broadens both its readability and potential influence with policy makers, educators, and the general public, a diverse audience that includes legislators, college trustees, school board members, and business and civic leaders. Without major changes in the reward system in higher education—affecting appointment, tenure, and promotion—there is little chance for meaningful and sustained change and involvement in K–12 issues. We refer here to universitywide policies because collaborative efforts ought not be limited to the faculties of schools of education.

Such questions as the following are raised for public discussion and debate in this report: How can those to whom it matters gain policy recognition of an issue as variegated, inchoate, and diffuse as k–12/higher education relationships? How can they get the attention of such interested parties as the financial aid community, the National Conference of State Legislatures (NCSL), and the National Governors Association (NGA)? What role should be played by such influential business groups as the Committee for Economic Development (CED), the National Alliance of Business (NAB), and the Business Roundtable (BRT)? What leverage points can be used at the national, state, and local levels to stimulate discussion and engage the appropriate policy makers? Our final chapter will explicitly address these vital questions.

Five Lenses for Viewing School–College Collaboration

This book represents one of the first mappings of the K–16 policy arena in readily accessible terms. The case studies emphasize established programs occurring throughout the country that have a direct impact on schools and student learning. They are categorized around major substantive issues that were selected to attain programmatic variety as well as diverse geographic representation. The five major interlevel themes provide a useful framework around which to study and develop policies for school–college collaboration. The cases fit into these five discrete, albeit at times overlapping, rubrics:

1. Governance
2. Equity
3. Standards
4. Teachers
5. Community building

In resisting the need to reexamine the structure of American education, too many policy makers fail to seize on advantages that might be derived by integrating more of the *governance* mechanisms of the school and college sectors. Such a change could certainly do more to produce the seamless connection that receives so much lip service. We look at cases in Massachusetts and Colorado. During the last decades of the 1900s, interest in *equity* became a burning issue that drove many of the interlevel initiatives. Our studies examine efforts in California, Tennessee, and Texas. The full force of the emergence of the *standards* movement during the 1990s makes this a logical area for collaboration. But unless those who set policies for schools and colleges can find better ways of working together, attempts to raise academic standards may come to naught, thwarted by disconnections between the two sectors. The ventures to bridge these disconnections that we study are in Maryland, Oregon, and Georgia. Simmering frustration over *teacher* quality, which until recently was focused on elementary and secondary schools, finally has led to increased attention to teacher education itself. Problems attendant to teacher quality will not be solved unless the two sides join in a mutual crusade, as we try to show in cases in Ohio and Mississippi. Finally, self-interest, even more than altruism, has brought institutions of higher education to recognize that their fates are ineluctably linked to those of the neighborhoods in which they are embedded. Elementary and secondary schools, some just blocks away from a college or university, as well as the higher education institutions themselves, can gain greatly from *community building* designed to revitalize neighborhoods. Our exemplary cases are in Connecticut and Pennsylvania.

Pressures for Change

Demographic changes that are reshaping the United States in profound ways will also shape the development of interlevel relationships between schools and colleges. With up to one-third of children under age 6 growing up in poverty or in economically marginal circumstances, the K–12 system is confronting serious social as well as educational challenges. The dramatic increase in the diversity of the population, with growing numbers of low-income, non-English-speaking youngsters, adds to the challenge. The pressure to strengthen K–16 transition policies has been further intensified by remediation costs in postsecondary institutions. In 1995, for example, nearly all public 2-year institutions and 81% of public 4-year institutions offered remedial courses in basic subjects such as English and math, and 29% of all freshmen were enrolled in at least one remedial class. If public school standards were elevated, of course, these remedial costs would not have to be borne by the postsecondary sector. The mutual stake of both sectors in ameliorating this situation is obvious, as is the public interest in eliminating the needless expense of course duplication in basic subjects that should be learned long before a student's college years.

We see only the tip of the demographic iceberg in the affirmative action debate as it manifests itself in California, Texas, and other states. Higher education has a massive stake in the quality of K–12 education, not only in terms of its provision of a pipeline of qualified students but also in preserving itself as an essential citadel of opportunity for growing numbers of underserved citizens in an increasingly pluralistic democracy. If equality of educational opportunity can be achieved in K–12, there will be less need for affirmative action or costly remedial strategies in higher education.

Interlevel relationships will develop in the years ahead also in the context of significant shifts in our intergovernmental system. Although student aid and research will continue to receive substantial federal support, there is little question that such other major areas as finance and governance will be state-oriented. Policy debates in these and other areas will continue to center in state capitals. The national emphasis will be on economic growth and competitiveness in a global economy, which will, in turn, generate a continuing focus on the education, skills, and training of Americans. Higher education and K–12 have common cause here and could potentially mount potent coalitions to work with the private sector as well as with political leaders to push an agenda stressing economic growth through education. Indeed, the pervasive concerns about economic competitiveness could be the lever to intensify efforts to work toward, in the words of John Goodlad of the University of Washington, a "simultaneous revival" of K–12 and postsecondary education as one seamless, continuous learning system.

Levers for Stimulating Coordination

A number of major interlevel issues potentially might serve as levers for changing the tenor of relationships. For example, the lack of congruence in so many places between the expanding state standards movement and college admissions practices might trigger some action. Indeed, with the erosion of support for affirmative action, admissions policy could well become high politics for governors and legislators. The lack of interlevel articulation in transition policies from twelfth grade to the freshman year and in assessment standards leaves a huge void in current reform strategies. Unless this situation is remedied, high school students will continue to be exposed to mixed and confusing signals, what Michael Kirst of Stanford University calls "a babble of standards, rather than a coherent strategy."

The public's growing concern about the quality of K–12 education will ensure that teacher education will remain a focus of interlevel relationships. Higher education institutions will be under growing pressure to improve their teacher preparatory programs. This obviously will entail closer working relationships with school systems. The national focus on the need to find 2 million capable new teachers in the next decade and the growing recognition of the centrality of teacher quality to efforts to improve and reform schools will inexorably focus attention on the deficiencies of so many teacher education programs on college campuses.

Many believe that the age of accountability is dawning for higher education, as it has already for K–12. Higher education may find to its surprise and chagrin that it faces accountability issues somewhat similar to those that have confronted its K–12 counterparts in recent years. There has been, for example, very little measurement of outcomes in postsecondary education. Dropout rates are extraordinarily high, and the blame cannot be placed exclusively on K–12. Indeed, the latter as well as the public at large are unaware of the diversity and qualitative unevenness of higher education and its attendant problems of high dropout rates and low achievement. A major challenge in the years ahead may well be to make higher education more accountable without undermining public confidence, as has happened somewhat unwittingly in K–12. As the accountability issue confronts the postsecondary sector, its stake in and dependence on improving the quality of K–12 education will become even more apparent.

It might be time to float radical ideas about the fundamental roles and missions of our educational institutions. We would be derelict if we did not mention the profound impact that technology can eventually have on interlevel relationships. The information revolution will provide opportunities for new modes of interaction and electronic connections between schools and colleges, though it is unclear what form these modes will take. The potential of technology obviously must be on the agenda of any efforts to promote interlevel cooperation in the years ahead.

These and other important issues will provide policy makers at all educational levels with crucial opportunities to place a higher priority on developing interlevel cooperation. There is an immediate need at the local, state, and national levels to generate cross-sector convening activities and to build a literature base in such a virginal policy realm. Boundary-spanning, catalytic activities ought to be initiated and strategic alliances and networks mobilized at all levels.

There also is the concomitant need to convene "big conversations" that are unfettered by constituency constraints and that transcend more limited local, state, regional, and professional perspectives. There is a tacit or latent frustration with the lack of interlevel cooperation or communication that could ultimately negatively impact both levels of education. Thus, there is a growing need for the organizations of state higher education executive officers and chief state school officers, as well as other relevant groups, to interact more regularly. No natural forum or mechanism exists under whose responsibility such necessary interlevel discussions occur on a systematic basis.

This situation may be changing somewhat as state-oriented stakeholders become more cognizant of the growing saliency of interlevel issues. A meeting at Stanford University in the fall of 1999, for example, focused on the central role of the state in creating closer relations between K–12 and higher education. This institute was held under the aegis of the National Conference of State Legislatures in conjunction with the Consortium for Policy Research in Education, the Education Commission of the States, and the Institute for Educational Leadership. Legislative leaders from 15 states attended. New federal legislation also illustrates escalating interest in the interlevel issue. The U.S. Department of Education, for example, in its recently enacted New Hopes Program, generates new connections between middle schools and postsecondary institutions by focusing on providing special academic enrichment offerings and support services designed to facilitate opportunities for economically disadvantaged youth.

The time is right for a more systematic and systemic approach to interlevel initiatives. Some of these issues facing policy makers have been alluded to in recent reports. The National Research Council, for example, in "Transforming Undergraduate Education in Science, Mathematics, Engineering and Technology," called on colleges and universities to serve more assertively as catalysts in efforts to improve K–12 math, science, and technology instruction. This can be accomplished, the report said, not only by raising admissions standards but also by sending clearer signals about the substantive preparation required in these disciplines. Other publications have also focused attention on the need for closer interlevel relationships, decrying the inertia that characterizes attitudes toward the issue in both the K–12 and postsecondary sectors.[2] What we offer in this report is a formulation that we hope provides some necessary stimulation for overcoming that inertia and the dysfunction that it breeds.

Notes

1. This opening chapter draws heavily on a recent article, "Two Different Worlds," by Patrick M. Callan and Michael D. Usdan in the *American School Board Journal*, December 1999, pp. 44–46.
2. See, for example, the first three documents in the publication series, "Perspectives in Public Policy: Connecting Higher Education and Public Schools," co-

sponsored by the National Center for Public Policy and Higher Education and the Institute for Educational Leadership: (1) *All One System: A Second Look*, by Harold L. Hodgkinson (June 1999); *Doing Comparatively Well: Why the Public Loves Higher Education and Criticizes K–12*, by John Immerwahr (October 1999); and *Higher Education and the Schools*, by P. Michael Timpane (December 1999).

PART I

Governance

One of the largely unexplored areas of collaboration between schools and colleges involves the integration of their governance. It would seem, after all, that if they could draw closer in their governance, perhaps even merging some aspects of their operations, it might be easier to grapple with some of the overlapping educational issues that are faced on both sides of the divide.

In what is perhaps one of the most ambitious examples of an institution of higher education involving itself in the governance of elementary and secondary schools, Boston University (BU) has for about a decade lent its expertise to the operations of the public school system in nearby Chelsea, Massachusetts. Lee D. Mitgang began watching this effort in its very earliest years and returned in 1999 to see what had transpired. Interestingly, despite the magnitude of BU's involvement in Chelsea, it has attracted little attention from the national media.

Mitgang found a project that was fueled very extensively by the protean efforts of one man, John Silber, the former president of Boston University. By force of personality, Silber had insinuated the university into almost every aspect of the operations of the school system, which, for the most part, was eager for the outside assistance. Almost everything that could have been wrong in Chelsea was wrong when the partnership with BU began. That is not to say that everyone welcomed the partnership; some teachers and others were quite skeptical of the arrangement. Persistence and hard work on both sides appear to have made a difference. Today, Chelsea would not be mistaken for the affluent suburbs of Newton or Lexington, but many aspects of the school system have changed for the better, and Silber and Boston University deserve a good deal of the credit. Yet the silence coming from other universities around the country that might seek to emulate BU is deafening.

At about the same time that BU and Chelsea joined forces, a different kind of alliance, with a less substantial impact, was effected in Pueblo, Colorado. In this instance, Public School District 60 and the University of Southern Colorado drew closer in their operations. The university attracted more than half of its students from the school system and recognized its stake in the school system. In its idealistic origin, this was to be a kind of merger, but the result was not a true merger. Janet and Sam Bingham and Dave Curtin found that efforts to share administrators or combine operations faced a clash of organizational cultures, disincentives to participate, and ambiguous leadership. The major results of the alliance have been programs to provide college courses to high school seniors, to improve science and math instruction, to create a charter school on the university campus, to promote relations between student teachers and university faculty, and to deliver better health care to public school students by using the university nursing students.

CHAPTER I

THE BOSTON UNIVERSITY–
CHELSEA PARTNERSHIP

Lee D. Mitgang

On a sun-drenched day in June 1999, 165 graduating seniors at Chelsea High School were serenaded by an unprepossessing, 13-member marching band outside the school's new home, an ultramodern building with spacious class-rooms, computer and language labs, and a well-stocked library. The hope-filled pageantry would have been unremarkable almost anywhere else. But here, across the Mystic River from Boston, it was tangible evidence of a unique rescue effort by a private university of an entire collapsing urban system where only 10 years earlier the music had died, children attended crumbling, cen-tury-old schools, and hope had been nearly extinguished by decades of de-cline and mismanagement.

In June 1989, Boston University (BU) and its then-president, John L. Silber, had accepted an invitation from the Chelsea School Committee to manage its failing school system. At the heart of the unprecedented partner-ship was a mandate from the locally elected committee for Boston Univer-sity to establish a management team with authority to govern all aspects of Chelsea's schools, from developing curriculum to hiring and firing adminis-trators to negotiating union contracts. The School Committee would retain oversight and could overrule the management team's decisions or even end the partnership by majority vote. But the university's management team and its hand-picked administrators would be firmly in charge of the day-to-day governance of Chelsea's schools for the next decade.

Colleges and universities across the country have operated individual ele-mentary schools—often as so-called laboratory schools for research by their professors and student teaching by their undergraduates. But the Boston University–Chelsea partnership has gone far beyond such town–gown acts of beneficence. The university, located 5 miles away in the prosperous Back Bay section of Boston, had no obvious stake in Chelsea's well-being. Beyond that, the university's reform blueprint for Chelsea would have been daring even for a state or the federal government to undertake.

Throughout the 1990s, the university handled the management of an educationally and financially bankrupt urban school district. More than this, it channeled a hefty portion of its energy, expertise, resources, and fund-raising clout for an all-out war on the educational, social, and health pathologies affecting children growing up in poor homes where, often, little English was spoken. Faculty from virtually every corner of Boston University—the schools of education, dentistry, management, public health, liberal arts, social work, and music—would end up volunteering their time and talent for no extra pay to the Chelsea partnership. Not least, the university would assume the costly task of renovating or replacing Chelsea's crumbling schools and lifting the salaries and professionalism of local teachers and administrators.

Boston University and Silber succeeded in attracting hundreds of millions of dollars in new state funding for the Chelsea public schools. "A Different September Foundation," established in 1991 by Silber to attract private donations for Chelsea, raised $9.7 million from corporations, individuals, and foundations by 1999, including a $2-million challenge grant from the Annenberg Foundation that helped revive music and art programs. Beyond its outside fund-raising, the university itself would contribute upwards of $10 million in in-kind services and expertise over the next decade.

Under the partnership, the Boston University management team established programs for adult home literacy and comprehensive health and dental care for underserved children and teens. At the heart of the university's plans were preschool programs aimed at ensuring school readiness for children growing up in educationally disadvantaged settings. In 1997, the partnership opened an Early Learning Center offering children as young as 4 a wholesome, stimulating place to spend their days while their parents worked. By 1999, nearly 1,000 Chelsea preschool and kindergarten children attended programs at the center, making it the largest in Massachusetts. "This is a total-exposure partnership," says Douglas Sears, a former assistant to Silber and Chelsea's superintendent since 1995. "You needed a nut like Silber to do it."

Indeed, from the beginning, the cocksure, iconoclastic Silber was the plan's energizing force, as well as the lightning rod for its many critics in education and politics. During a long career in higher education, Silber had lifted the national stature of Boston University, but his tough talk against teacher unions and his occasional scorn for fellow college presidents earned him his share of detractors. Some suggested that universities had no business managing school districts and that Silber's line between community service and self-aggrandizement seemed at times thinly drawn. Silber routinely dismissed such criticisms, countering that for a university to operate a school district was no less appropriate than a university with a medical school to run a hospital: "We are not ashamed to be caught in service to our community. In fact, we believe that's one of the functions of universities. That's one of the reasons we merit support. And we might as well get it straight that a university is a public institution whether it is supported by a city, or the state, or by the private sector. We are a public institution."

Desperation in Chelsea

On Chelsea's side, the idea for the partnership was born of desperation. Through the first half of the twentieth century, this once-proud community's schools had a reputation for excellence, guiding Irish, Polish, Italian, and Jewish immigrants to college, good jobs, and, as often as not, comfortable lives in places beyond Chelsea. By the 1980s, decades of demographic changes, incompetent management, nepotism, and neglect had left the school system in ruins. Test scores, graduation rates, and teacher salaries ranging from $17,300 for beginners to $30,320 for the few with doctorates were among the state's lowest. Educational leadership was almost nonexistent: What passed for a curriculum before the partnership was defined largely by the abilities and caprices of each teacher. Suzanne H. Chapin, an associate professor at BU's School of Education specializing in math education, described the chaotic atmosphere in the first days of the partnership: "There were no goals or objectives, no consistent textbook series. There was very little leadership, and little connecting with other colleagues. Many were uncertified in math instruction. Teachers would tell us in November, 'I haven't gotten around to teaching math yet.' Principals were screaming at teachers, teachers were screaming at children. I sometimes went home and cried."

Art and music had nearly disappeared from the schools. By 1989, fewer than half of the pupils entering Chelsea High School graduated, and fewer than one in five planned to attend a 4-year college. Only 24% took the SAT; 59%, many from Hispanic or Southeast Asian backgrounds, lacked adequate grounding in the English language. One in four girls was pregnant or already a mother. The city itself had little commerce, a decrepit housing stock, and a shrinking tax base. Per-pupil spending on schools ranked near the bottom in the state. The newest school in town was built in 1909, and some were more than a century old. The playgrounds were unsafe, there were no cafeterias, and slate was falling from roofs. In common with many urban districts with large enrollments of immigrants, student mobility was incredibly high: more than one-third of the student population transferred into or out of the district each year. As much as anything else, the high mobility rate would continually frustrate efforts at achieving dramatic or durable improvements in standardized test scores and other yardsticks of school progress over the next decade.

Chelsea, in short, was a district in search of a messiah, and Silber was eager to assume the role. Several years earlier, he had brashly offered to manage Boston's schools, only to be rebuffed. When Andrew Quigley, a local newspaper publisher who was a member of the Chelsea School Committee, and John Brennan, who was Chelsea's mayor, approached Silber about managing their failing schools, he leapt at the challenge. He promptly assigned a team to diagnose the ills of Chelsea's schools, an assignment that led to a 231-page action plan.

The resulting blueprint was not merely one of the most ambitious efforts ever undertaken to resuscitate blighted schools and improve the lives of poor children. It was also a calculated affront to the education establishment and much of the prevailing wisdom of progressive urban education. The results in the decade ahead would be a dizzying mix of improvements in student performance, political and legal battles, unforeseen crises and disappointments, and more curiosity than support from others in higher education.

To be sure, the reform plan contained enticements for teachers: rich opportunities for professional development including full and partial scholarships at Boston University, along with badly needed across-the-board pay increases to lift salaries to more competitive levels. But the BU management team also deliberately broke with orthodoxy by hiring superintendents and principals with few traditional educational credentials to go with leadership skills demonstrated in noneducational fields. Whole-language reading instruction, embraced by "progressive" educators, was replaced by an early childhood curriculum heavy on phonics. Hand calculators, which had come into vogue in the 1980s when the National Council of Teachers of Mathematics conferred its blessing on them, yielded to more traditional drill and memorization of math basics. Teacher contracts included generous across-the-board raises, but also provisions for longer hours and merit pay that unions had long resisted. Most controversially in this district, where roughly two-thirds of pupils are Hispanic, Silber embarked on a bilingual educational program, stressing as its goal English proficiency at an early age.

Silber's steamroller style and his frontal attacks on local politicians and unions meant that not everyone in Chelsea rejoiced at the prospect of handing the keys to Boston University's experts. He reminisced about his early battles with teachers' unions and principals: "We just told the principals, 'go ahead and strike. We'll take your strike and replace every damn one of you.' We weren't inhibited about getting rid of incompetent principals. We also had it out with the teachers' union, and we regained most of the management rights that had been given away. That's what needs to be said all across this country to the teachers' union."

Long-time school committeewoman Elizabeth McBride, who eventually became an ardent backer of the partnership, opposed it in 1988 on political principle: "I didn't think the School Committee should turn over its authority to any private institution," she said. "Isn't that what democracy is about?" Many Spanish-speakers were alarmed by Silber's views on bilingual education, feeling his stance belittled their language and culture. The local teachers' union joined other early foes in trying unsuccessfully to block the plan in court. Veteran Chelsea teachers and school administrators also bristled at what they perceived as a know-it-all attitude about classroom practices and curricula on the part of some university professors, literally turning their backs on faculty members when they first arrived in Chelsea to demonstrate different teaching methods.

"What happened was you had theoreticians talking to practitioners, and the two don't necessarily mix," said Carol Murphy, director of Chelsea's Early Learning Center and one of the few survivors of the early purges of Chelsea's principals and administrators. "Sometimes what the BU faculty thought was going to work in the classrooms, didn't. They taught classes and fell flat on their faces, and it was humbling. It was only then that we were able to start working together."

A fresh disaster hit Chelsea in 1991. Just as the partnership was producing its first signs of progress, the local government was placed in state receivership because of a $9.5-million projected deficit. The collapse of Chelsea's finances abruptly turned the saviors from Boston into executioners. The BU management team was forced to eliminate 50 of 300 teaching positions. Class sizes ballooned to 40 students. Sports, physical education, and the scant remains of the art and music programs were further reduced or eliminated. Still, as devastating as those cuts were, the receivership turned out to be an opportunity to clear away much of the endemic nepotism and other political debris that might have eventually stymied the partnership's efforts. In time, many who originally opposed the partnership, including the teachers' union, grew to support it as signs of recovery mounted. Hard evidence of that growing cordiality came in 1997, a year before the partnership agreement was scheduled to expire, when the School Committee asked Boston University to renew the partnership for 5 more years to the 2002–2003 school year, and the university agreed.

Signs of Progress

Eleven years into the partnership, both sides point to numerous signs of progress. Teacher salaries have risen nearly 60% since 1988, to a range of $27,000 to $48,340 in 1999. Per-pupil spending increased by 75% during that period, from $4,055 before the partnership to $7,015 in fiscal 1999. The number of graduates was up from 133 in 1989 to 165 in 1999, and nearly three out of four had plans for postsecondary education, compared with 52% of graduates in 1989. Chelsea is no longer at the bottom among Massachusetts urban districts in test scores: Chelsea High sophomores stood 243rd statewide among 321 high schools in the 1998 Massachusetts Comprehensive Assessment System. A study that year by the University of Massachusett's Donohue Institute placed Chelsea at the top of a list of "noteworthy districts" where standardized test scores were below state averages but higher than expected given the district's demographic profile. On the other hand, test scores for younger pupils among Chelsea's 6,000 students have been less encouraging despite the partnership's heavy emphasis on early childhood learning. Third-grade Iowa literacy test scores in 1998 were in the 29th national percentile, the worst in the state, but rose to a still subpar 39 percent in 1999.

Despite the uneven progress that those numbers suggest, Chelsea is no longer the pariah among Massachusetts districts. Favorable impressions of Chelsea's schools are now such that more than 100 pupils from neighboring towns such as Revere were discovered in 1998 to have given false residency information in order to attend Chelsea's schools. The most visible testament to the partnership are the new or renovated school buildings throughout Chelsea, including the showcase high school opened in 1996. Silber pried loose some $115 million in state school construction dollars, leveraging his many friendships with legislators, to renovate or replace every school building in the district, at virtually no cost to the district. The new buildings, 17-year-old senior Bettsaly Echevarria told a visitor, "make you want to go to school, and be proud of your school. I play interscholastic volleyball, and kids from other schools come here and say, 'Wow, we wish we could have schools like this.'"

It must be underscored that it was the state, not Boston University, that provided the critical funding allowing the management team to boost teacher salaries, update facilities, and buy new books, supplies, computers and other instructional materials. The state's Education Reform Act of 1993 sent an outpouring of state funds to urban districts as a result of equitable funding lawsuits. Yet it is also certain that the level of public and private support for Chelsea's schools would never have approached the sums reached during the 1990s were it not for Silber's political savvy and connections.

Apart from the rise in test scores, there has been a palpable improvement in the atmosphere in Chelsea's classrooms and corridors. When Lincoln Tamayo, a tough-talking Silber protégé with a law degree and a master's in education from Harvard but no traditional credentials as a secondary school administrator, was installed as principal of Chelsea High in July 1996, the climate was so threatening that the dean of students was afraid to go to the bathroom. Students with hats, beepers, and Walkmen aimlessly roamed the halls, and average daily attendance was less than 80%. Tamayo, whose computer screen-saver flashes the message NO EXCUSES!, has begun revitalizing the school with an uncompromising behavior and attendance code and an emphasis on academic standards. Days after he took over, 100 students walked out of school to protest his new rules. Tamayo gave them 5 minutes to return to classes or be declared trespassers. Half returned; half continued their protest at City Hall. But the message was received. Of the 13 students who took Advanced Placement (AP) tests in 1996, only 2 scored 3 or 4 on a scale of 5, the levels needed to get credit from most colleges later on. By 1999, 83 took AP exams, and 27 earned scores of 3 or higher. Daily attendance had also improved by 1999, to a still-subpar 90%.

What Boston University Gained

If Chelsea was the desperate partner with much to gain and little to lose, what did the partnership hold for Boston University besides the huge investment in time, treasure, and the potential risks to its reputation? Along with his convictions about community service, Silber argues that the arrangement has paid dividends for his university's school of education: "You couldn't imagine a first-rate medical school if it didn't have an affiliation with a hospital. I don't see having a first-rate school of education if you don't have a really close, intimate affiliation with a school system. Of course it's a benefit to the university in that sense."

The Boston University–Chelsea partnership also afforded participating faculty opportunities for research and the resulting publications on what works in urban school reform. Since 1997, for example, Professor Chapin has gotten three federal research grants totaling more than $775,000 related to her work with Chelsea math teachers and has published more than half a dozen related scholarly works. Such scholarly activity is a matter of some delicacy, however, since university faculty also had to convince Chelsea's school community that their involvement was not motivated by profit or professional advancement.

Whatever the motives or potential inducements, the fact is that other institutions of higher learning have not followed BU's wide-ranging, all-encompassing example, nor have any expressed serious interest in doing so. The reasons are not mysterious: Asking whether the BU–Chelsea arrangement is a replicable school reform model for other colleges to adopt is a bit like asking whether Evel Kneivel's Grand Canyon motorcycle jump was a wise model for the average couch potato to follow. Immersing a university for more than a decade in the management, politics, and finances of a failing school district—and all the while waging war on the prevailing curricular and pedagogical beliefs of the education establishment—are not for the faint-hearted. Still, the record logged in Chelsea during the first 11 years of the partnership suggests that the university's governance experiment cannot be dismissed as a foolhardy leap across the abyss.

The explanation for why other colleges and universities have not yet followed the example of the Boston University–Chelsea partnership certainly relates to the personality of Silber himself. If the occasionally unkind caricature of the typical college president portrays a person mainly preoccupied with raising money, refereeing parking disputes, and keeping his school and himself out of controversy, few would dispute that Silber is the polar opposite. Simply put, he may prove to be the only leader in higher education with the requisite surpluses of boldness, social commitment, and gall to commit an entire university to the long-term salvaging of an urban school district. Beyond personalities, the most obvious lessons from Boston University's experiences are that to be truly effective, reform plans must be comprehensive, touching all aspects of school and home life. The human and financial commitment that that implies from a university community, along with the decade or more it would take to show real and durable progress, suggests that this school reform and governance model, while potentially effective, will almost certainly remain rare. Indeed, the 10-year duration of the Chelsea plan originally projected by Silber seems overly optimistic if not naive in retrospect.

Some of the more subtle lessons learned the hard way, according to participants on both sides, include the need for building trust and a true sense of partnership from the start. Motivations from the beginning must be straightforward and unambiguous: Nearly everyone agrees that the decision by BU to make participation by faculty purely voluntary and uncompensated was a wise one. Professor Lee Indrisano, a senior Boston University education school faculty member, adds that a vital aspect of the Chelsea plan that evolved later in its history was the decision to provide incentives for Chelsea teachers to become team leaders and researchers. Any such plan, Indrisano says, should train and nurture classroom teachers to become active participants in designing the reform plans and in helping fellow teachers discover new and better classroom methods. In that way, a legacy of school change can be built and a sense of genuine partnership fostered.

Rightly or not, Silber also argues that an essential element of any university–school management agreement must be a willingness to face down teachers' unions, which too often have "stolen" management prerogatives, and to adopt what he regards as the "right" approaches to teaching math, English, and other basics. He elaborates: "The first thing I'd say is, 'What kind of school of education do you have?' If they said we don't have one, I'd say, good, you're ahead of the game. If you have one, it better be like Boston University's, which hasn't sold out to a lot of politically correct nonsense. If you've got a school that's teaching whole language, don't touch the schools because you'll only hurt them. If you have people who say that in order to teach mathematics to young children we want to give them calculators, then stay away from public education because all you'll do is hurt these children's chances. But if you have a good school of education that requires most of its student to spend their time in subject courses—mathematics, English, history—then that's wonderful."

A key unanswered question remains: when, and even whether, the management partnership should end. Silber sees no reason why the university wouldn't agree to continue the partnership indefinitely if asked. Many in Chelsea dread the June 2003 scheduled end of the partnership, fearing that the corruption, nepotism, and mismanagement that hastened Chelsea's downfall are still waiting in the wings. "It will be a sad day when the partnership ends," says Guy Santagate, Chelsea's city manager. But others wonder if the musculature of self-governance and community involvement in Chelsea might permanently atrophy if the partnership continued indefinitely. Despite improvements in Chelsea's educational climate, the partnership has made little headway in generating citizen activism. School Committee and management team meetings are open to the public, but apart from a highly contested decision to distribute condoms at Chelsea High in 1991, such meetings have been poorly attended.

It may be, then, that the partnership will have passed one of its most important tests as a national model of school reform when Chelsea's School Committee and citizenry feel confident enough in themselves and their future to tell Boston University and John Silber, "Thanks. We can take it from here."

CHAPTER 2

An Alliance in Pueblo

Janet Bingham, Sam Bingham, and Dave Curtin

The suggestion emerged in a 1990 brainstorming session among university and public school educators in Pueblo, Colorado. If the school district and the college that received its graduates and trained its teachers joined forces, wouldn't the richer community generate better ideas to raise performance and cut costs for both institutions? Both the local school board and the State Board of Agriculture, which oversees the University of Southern Colorado (USC), embraced the idea without reservation and signed a formal agreement vowing to work together. In 1991 the superintendent of Pueblo School District 60 became simultaneously vice-president of the University of Southern Colorado, and the Educational Alliance of Pueblo was born. Education reformers had long talked about improving student learning by creating a seamless system of education from kindergarten through college graduation, the so-called K–16 concept now getting attention around the country. Pueblo was among the first communities in the country to establish a formal framework to reach that goal.

"The idea was that we had a lot to gain by working together," said Robert Shirley, who was then president of the university. Both the time and the place seemed propitious. Pueblo is a steel mill town of 100,000, ethnically and culturally diverse, determined to rekindle civic pride and prosperity in a postindustrial economy. Enrollment in Pueblo School District 60 had been sliding due to the city's economic situation. District officials were keenly aware of the need to reverse high dropout rates and low average student performance. Of the district's 18,000 students, about half are Hispanic and about half qualify for subsidized lunches. The university has a strong community presence and convenient location. Nearly 60% of its 4,200 resident students come from District 60 schools, and a majority of the district's teachers have degrees from USC. The university and the school district are symbiotic, in that the success of each depends on the other. The decline in school district enrollment meant a decline in university enrollment would inevitably follow. Both the university and the district were preparing to update their strategic planning in the interest of greater financial efficiency and higher academic performance.

The experiment has survived to see the new millennium. On a blustery fall day at the beginning of the 1999–2000 school year, future elementary school teachers in a science program were out for a behind-the-scenes trip to the city zoo. The science curriculum for future teachers, put together by eight USC professors and six public school teachers, integrates physics, chemistry, biology, ecology, geology, and other disciplines "because that's how science is taught in elementary school," said Jack Seilheimer, dean of the College of Science and Mathematics at USC. And, indeed, as the participants huddled in an operating room big enough to accommodate a sick camel, they grilled zoo veterinarian Norman Armentrout on subjects students might raise in the classroom. "How does a group of primates handle the death of a member? Can animal diseases be transmitted to humans? What happens to the mothering instinct when a zebra foal dies at birth?" And math questions— How many pounds of meat does a lion consume? How many gallons of water? How many square feet of space does it need? What does it cost? "Teacher candidates study how to prep kids for a trip to the zoo and what they should get out of it," said Oralia Gil, a District 60 K–6 teacher resource assistant who also teaches the class of USC seniors.

Seilheimer said the Alliance has cut red tape for university faculty members and district teachers who want to work together to create a seamless curriculum and bridge the gap between the two institutions. It has boosted awareness, he said, that both sides are all in the same business: educating the community's children. But not everyone has bought into the concept. The science–math linkage emerged as one of the few shining stars in the Alliance. Even the strongest supporters admit that the Alliance has yet to realize its full potential. Critics say it exists mainly on paper. While a 1997 State of Colorado audit recommended continuing the Alliance, it has not become a model for replication in Colorado, or almost anywhere else, for that matter. It remains, as it was in the beginning, a learning experience for reasons perhaps more implicit in the mundane details than in the concept.

The original structure that gave the school superintendent a strong position in the university administration did not create a true merger. The two institutions, by contract, remained autonomous, governed by separate boards. The 5-member district board is elected by Pueblo residents, while the 9-member State Board of Agriculture, which oversees the university, is appointed by the governor. When the Alliance was created, an additional 11-member board was set up to oversee joint activities with input from an advisory council comprising teachers from each of the district's 32 schools and faculty from each college and department at the university. There is also a national advisory board, which is worth mentioning as a measure of the interest that the Alliance generated among education reformers across the country. Its original 14 members included the late T. H. Bell, a former Secretary of the U.S. Department of Education; Henry Cisneros, who would become a Secretary of the U.S. Department of Housing and Urban Development; Keith Geiger, who was then president of the National Education Association; and the late Albert Shanker, who was then president of the American Federation of Teachers.

The Alliance has touched both academic and support activities at the operational level, including the following academic programs:

- *The Senior to Sophomore Program* provided USC courses with fully transferable credits to high school seniors.
- *Curriculum Articulation in the Sciences* involved joint programs to improve science and math instruction and student performance. Five grants totaling about $1.2 million have provided support since inception. After three of these ended, the program was continued under the regular budget.
- *The Pueblo School for the Arts and Sciences (PSAS)*, a K–12 college-oriented charter school on the USC campus, was also intended to serve as a laboratory school for the University teacher education department and its students.
- *The Center for Teaching, Learning, and Research* was a vehicle for involving USC faculty and student teachers in the school system and vice versa. It was also intended to provide pre-service and in-service training for USC education students and district teachers.
- *The Nursing Linkage* delivered health benefits for district students while providing real-world experience for USC nursing students.

Other academic linkages were initiated but failed to develop, including a teacher exchange program, joint research, and a mentoring program on the model of Big Brothers/Big Sisters. Supporting amalgamations have included an Alliance Grants Center for collaborative grant writing and a Technology Partnership to coordinate computer networks between the district and the university. A Business Services Partnership includes a combined purchasing office, a combined safety office (overseeing compliance with regulations), and combined printing services. An effort was also made to place facilities maintenance under joint management.

Making the Alliance More Than a Symbol

In retrospect, however, it seems clear that the relatively symbolic nature of the Alliance structure was too weak to maintain collaboration in some cases and probably not necessary to initiate it in others. Such activities as the Curriculum Articulation in the Sciences continue to get rave reviews. Others, like the Senior to Sophomore Program and the Nursing Linkage, could have come about without the joint board or the superintendent's university vice-presidency. The technology partnership originally entertained ambitious plans for computer networking, but after rewiring several schools it was able to generate few collaborative projects because the district and university have different computer systems. The national advisory board of all-star educational reformers hasn't met for 2 years. Because of a loss of momentum, the logistics and expense of getting the educational heavyweights together could not be justified. The Grants Center brought in $3 million during the first 6 years—as long as the spirit of the Alliance remained focused and compelling. But in time the separate needs and conventions of the district and the university reimposed themselves. "Grants are supposed to buy people the time to reflect and change. Instead, people used them to do more of what they were doing with more money as opposed to eventually doing it differently with the same amount," said former director David Trujillo. After a district employee was assigned to look after district interests, the allied office began to lose its meaning and was eventually discontinued.

In both academic and nonacademic areas, efforts to share administrators or combine operations faced difficulties because of a clash of organizational cultures, disincentives to participate, and ambiguous leadership. Bureaucratic feathers were ruffled with the appointment of the district deputy superintendent as dean of the Center for Teaching, Learning, and Research. "It was fairly controversial having university faculty reporting to an administrator who was a full-time official in the school district," said ex-president Shirley. And from the standpoint of the deputy superintendent, wearing two full-time hats added up to an enormous amount of work. A full-time director, based at the university, has recently been hired to manage day-to-day operations.

Shared building maintenance foundered because different pay scales, titles, and employee evaluations created conflict whenever workers from both institutions worked side by side on the same job. After 18 months on the job, joint facilities manager Ed Smith wrote in a 1993 Alliance newsletter: "District employees felt there was enough work in the 34 school buildings to keep them busy. They had little inclination to go to the university, especially since USC employees earned about 15% more for similar work. On the other hand, university employees believed that district workers would take over their jobs. Even the best idea could be consumed in politics. Employees who chose to fight the process could do so through inaction, by asking lots of questions or by involving the union. In many ways the local unions perceived the Alliance as a management-concocted threat."

Former district superintendent Henry Roman, who retired in June 1999, lamented that the state personnel system that governs the universities is extremely inflexible and that the school district unions are extremely protective of their work forces. Shirley had hoped that shared administrative positions and combined operations would save money that could be put back into the classroom. But the 1997 state audit found that while "the benefits of the Alliance generally outweigh the related costs," the financial effects were less than expected.

The main impact came at the outset. The university and the district worked together in 1991 to make major changes in the district's organization. About 7.5% of the district's general fund budget was reallocated from noninstructional to instructional purposes. The reallocation was accomplished through streamlining central administration, closing two schools, privatizing some services, and integrating some administrative functions with USC. The money went into a special fund that has fluctuated over the years. The allocation in the fall of 1999 was about $3.4 million. Of that, $2.1 million a year goes to individual schools; the rest is used for districtwide instructional programs, including some Alliance activities. Direct savings credited to the Alliance itself have been modest. These resulted primarily from consolidation of a couple of positions and some operations such as purchasing and the print shop. According to the state audit, off-setting costs for Alliance activities left a net gain of only about $60,000, although many costs and savings turned out to be difficult to quantify, given overlapping budgets and responsibilities.

The importance of the Alliance thus rests on its impact on programs rather than on finances, and here, too, the verdict remains tentative. The auditors' "concerns . . . regarding the lack of clear, complete data about costs, benefits, and use of savings" were followed by comments on a widespread ambiguity among employees of both partners as well as in the wider community as to what the Alliance really stood for. Was it an organization responsible for programs and activities or merely an "agreement"? Communication efforts had focused on promoting it, but what exactly was it? Also, the Alliance had never announced any criteria for measuring progress. Two years later, critics both inside and outside the partner institutions continue to voice similar concerns. Fifth-grade teacher Suzanne Ethridge: "It's basically an alliance on paper, not a true partnership. There's no forum for collaboration and communication. We've started a program in the district to get teachers endorsed in English as a Second Language or get a master's degree in bilingual education and USC was supposed to have underwritten that, but it fell apart. Adams State College, 125 miles away, had to take over the program. With the Alliance, USC should be our partner in this, but no one wanted to take over the leadership." USC's inability to grant graduate degrees is a continuing issue.

Dealing with the Flaws

Most critics stop short of calling for an end to the experiment. Trujillo, who ran the Alliance Grants Center, still believes the idea is "brilliant." But he said that Shirley's hope that a structural linkage at the top would automatically foster creative collaboration throughout was flawed. "Bob had a forceful personality and a grasp of the political," Trujillo said. "He rushed into the concept because of an opportunity that presented itself." After Shirley retired in December 1996, the Alliance seemed to stagnate. Trujillo said: "No one owned it. The motivation was to make the two systems work as one system with the student's well-being at the center. I don't think that ever penetrated the policy, procedures, consciousness of the vast majority of practitioners on either side. It was one of those top-down innovations that people resent—whether it was good or not."

Trujillo now directs grants at New Jersey City University, but the experience in Pueblo has caused him, like many others, to reflect seriously on what, besides redrawing the organization charts, it takes to change the culture and direction of institutions, not to mention induce them to work together. "Maybe it's a matter of learning how to do it in a way that the K–12 folks aren't threatened, so the postsecondary folks don't act arrogant and know-it-all." Better incentives are needed, he said. "Implementation is the hard stuff: getting people to behave differently, looking at compensation and rewards. Why should university faculty work on K–16 partnerships when they get no reward? They're supposed to be working on research and publications and teaching their courses. Faculty who did participate were hammered for it. On the district side, the Alliance was viewed as more work, not as doing things differently."

High turnover of personnel at the upper echelons has plagued both partners. From 1991 through 1999 USC has seen three presidents (one acting) and District 60 four superintendents. "I don't mean to suggest any less fervor or commitment in the Alliance, but when there's a change in personnel, the newcomers are in a vertical learning curve," said current USC president Tito Guerrero, who took office in July 1997. Former school superintendent Henry Roman, who retired in June of 1999, says that the changing faces make it imperative for any educational alliance "to have a strong, overarching vision." Lacking that, the Alliance continues to rise and fall according to the enthusiasm of individual players in individual programs. District teachers who have embraced the opportunities say they have reaped the rewards.

Dianne Brooks, an English teacher at Centennial High, participates in the Senior to Sophomore Program. The 32 students in her English 102 class get credit at the university. The credits also transfer to other colleges. "I have to attend all the English Composition Department meetings at the university, but that's a big plus for me because I'm with people who really know what they're doing in the area of composition—people I wouldn't have access to if I weren't doing this," said Brooks. Her students also benefit from the Online Writing Laboratory. "Students can type an essay into their computer, e-mail it to the lab at the university, and get their paper back with suggestions from a tutor about how to make it better. That helps them, and it helps me a lot because by the time I get the paper, it's a better paper." Former deputy superintendent Joyce Bales, who oversaw the Center for Teaching, Learning, and Research under Shirley, is now superintendent of District 60. A new full-time director, Victoria Marquesen, is breathing new life into the Center. She recently landed a $3.7-million federal grant (one of 25 nationally) to prepare teacher candidates for work in districts where a high percentage of students come from low-income families, teacher turnover is historically high, and many teachers work outside their certified specialties. All members of Colorado's higher education system are under pressure to adapt teacher training to meet new state standards for the three Rs.

The Alliance's Impact

Unfortunately there is no statistical evidence that the Alliance has improved achievement or raised the number or quality of students applying to USC from District 60, although a clear cause-and-effect relationship would be difficult to show. When Bales came to the district in 1994, she found that many Pueblo District 60 graduates could not read well enough to function successfully at USC, and half of those who did enter could not pass the first semester of college algebra. In 1997, when Colorado administered its first statewide tests designed to measure student progress toward meeting new fourth-grade reading and writing standards, Pueblo's results placed it well below the state average. Bales has been determined to change that, and the state now requires districts to raise the pass rate by 25% over 3 years or lose accreditation.

The standard perception was that the university would lift the school district, but possibly the district will have a greater impact on the university.

Since 1997, largely through its own initiative, Pueblo District 60 has raised the fourth-grade pass rate in reading from 44% to 57%, a 30% gain in 3 years, while test scores statewide have remained stagnant. One school, Bessemer Elementary, has become the hands-down state champion for improved performance. It was an archetypal underachieving school—80% low-income and 80% Hispanic. Nevertheless, the fourth-graders meeting standards on the reading test jumped from 12% in 1997 to 64% in 1998 to 74% in 1999, far out-performing the Alliance's own charter school. Bessemer's comprehensive reading curriculum has drawn statewide attention, and the district offered training in the Lindamood-Bell reading technique during the summer of 1999 to teachers, university faculty members, and teacher education students. Bales is getting increasing requests from student teachers to learn the Bessemer model. Altogether, she said, university students have spent thousands of hours tutoring reading.

Bales believes that the Alliance does have a role to play. Referring to the Center for Teaching, Learning, and Research, she pointed out that in one school where a USC faculty member made weekly visits, test scores averaged a 10-point gain in four of six areas as students progressed from third grade to fourth and from fourth to fifth. Beginning in 1998, faculty members have been given 60 to 120 hours of released time to actually go and be part of the schools and work with principals and teachers. "There are a lot of things happening that wouldn't have happened if we hadn't made a commitment to the Alliance," Bales said. "It's a natural" for the district to work with the university's teacher preparation program, she noted. "We're the ones who employ them and serve as a training ground for student teachers. I want new teachers to be able to implement a standards-based curriculum, to understand and be able to use assessment information. There's a weakness at the university level in helping teachers understand assessments."

Does the Pueblo Alliance then deserve to be a model for other school districts and colleges? The state auditors did not say that this was the case. They found that the "current Alliance organization is . . . not necessary for other institutions to achieve benefits from cooperative efforts. . . . We found numerous cooperative efforts throughout the State that do not depend on an organization similar to the Alliance." One of these, the Pueblo Community Compact for Student Success, in fact joins both USC and Pueblo District 60 in a larger association that embraces the more suburban Pueblo District 70, Pueblo Community College, the Chamber of Commerce, and the Latino Chamber of Commerce. Funded by private grants for 7 years ending in 2000, it has also aimed at establishing a standards-based preK–16 education system. Though less ambitious in terms of organizational reform, it has no doubt contributed to an overall spirit of, and pressure for, collaboration.

Compact director LeeAnn Whithnell asserted that their goal has been to influence individual institutions rather than create a unified organization. "The Alliance was such a bold step! I happened to be in the school district at the time. People said, 'They're going to do what? Who's in charge?' There were all these turf issues. I think it set the foundation so change can happen, but just two organizations is too specific." She pointed out that Pueblo District 70, the semirural suburban district that surrounds Pueblo 60 like a doughnut, is as big as Rhode Island and has a role to play as well. Former District 60 superintendent Roman liked the tighter focus but does not believe the Alliance structure would work for a national institution. "If you tailor your programs to the needs of the local district, you lose sight of your other customers. USC is a regional university drawing 60% of its kids from Pueblo, and that's an important distinction." USC's Guerrero isn't so sure. "Any community that has a need to serve children could find a way to develop these kinds of alliances," he said.

After nearly a decade, the Pueblo Educational Alliance remains at best a work in progress without any guarantee that it will fulfill its promise as a way to build a dynamic and efficient K–16 system. Nevertheless, a harsh judgment of its impact would obscure the lessons it offers for the K–16 idea that is now getting attention in such states as Maryland and Georgia. If the integration of a school district and a local college can work anywhere, it is still hard to imagine a better place than Pueblo for trying it. USC serves primarily students in southern Colorado, and the university has an inherent interest in improving the education of students in the area. And since a large number of the teachers in the school district are graduates of USC, the district has an interest in ensuring that USC education students receive high-quality teacher training. Finally, the geographic proximity of the university and the district lends itself to interaction between employees of the two and contributes to their ability to share resources.

Nonetheless, the Pueblo experience offers some hard lessons. For starters, blending two institutions with different structures, different cultures, and less than 100% overlapping missions is not as simple as the founders of the Pueblo Alliance imagined. Making the school superintendent a vice-president at the university and issuing some plans and protocols isn't enough to work a spirit of shared purpose into the pores of either institution so deeply that collaboration becomes automatic. Even disparities at the most basic level—the varying pay scales of maintenance workers in each system, for example—are difficult to reconcile. But differences in intellectual orientation stress the system, too. Even a local institution such as USC has a much broader mission than just training teachers, and university professors, when they feel threatened, will guard their prerogatives. Creative tension is not an oxymoron, and a seamless union that strives to both accentuate the positive and eliminate the negative, as the old song says, may not be entirely possible or necessarily in the best interests of both systems.

The current pressure on both the school district and the university stemming from the national debate over educational standards will certainly have an effect on the Alliance and will keep it, even with its unfulfilled potential, in the spotlight. Pueblo District 60 is exactly the kind of school district that sparked the call for imposing measurable achievement goals, and its response in relation to the rest of Colorado is impressive. The remarkable advances at Bessemer Elementary School and general gains in reading and writing scores have caught the attention of the state's new governor and the media. It remains to be seen how much pressure the successes in the school system will put on the teacher education program at the university to serve an evolving "Pueblo Model." The Alliance structure could be a medium for this. On the other hand, momentum to implement a more uniform, standards-based approach throughout the district could cause at least some of the university staff to assert their independence more robustly. Versions of this little drama are apt to be played out throughout the United States, but they will be particularly interesting to watch in Pueblo as new leadership in both Pueblo District 60 and the University of Southern Colorado take up the challenges of the new millennium.

PART II

Equity

For some time now, questions have been raised about how the educational structure can promote equity, using learning and credentialing to help bring more Americans into the economic and social mainstream. It would seem that the more seamless the connections between precollegiate and collegiate education, the better the chances of realizing the goal of equity. When students reach higher education without the sort of preparation that will make success more likely, the outcome in college-level courses can be disastrous—if they even enter college.

Kenneth R. Weiss looked at collaborative efforts on behalf of equity in California, a state that is undergoing a historic shift in the composition of its K–12 enrollment, with ethnic minorities comprising a growing portion of the students. It is in the interests of both the students and the universities that these young people be equipped to prosper in postsecondary education. Toward these ends, both the University of California and California State University have fashioned programs to work more closely with elementary and secondary schools. The two university systems have taken different approaches, with somewhat different results. All this is complicated by taking place at a time when California is trying to raise academic standards. Weiss identified encouraging signs but hesitated to go so far as to say that the programs are working—which probably only time will tell.

In El Paso, operating on a smaller scale, the partnership between several school systems in the area and the University of Texas at El Paso has received more definitive praise for its results. Yet, as Duchesne Paul Drew noted, "Sustaining the Collaborative has been a continuous challenge to motivate and move a complex system with partners and situations that no single entity controls." Even in the most promising academic collaborations, as in El Paso, cultures must be meshed and egos must be cushioned to make anything happen in the first place and to keep it happening. Drew found that the venture in El Paso had favorable results because it was of manageable size, leaders were committed to real change, an accountability system created incentives, two foundations provided important extra funding, and attention was given simultaneously to several fronts.

Another kind of approach to equity is exemplified by the middle college high school concept, which began in New York City and spread across the country. This partnership in all instances involved putting a high school on a community college campus—close to role models and in the midst of an institution to which the high school students can aspire. The collaboration between the Memphis Public Schools and Shelby State Community College was studied by Mickie Anderson. She found a situation that endured very difficult early years because of the natural difficulties and certain miscalculations. Joyce Mitchell, the founding principal of the high school, said that if she had known what the project had in store for her, she might not even have applied for the job. Eventually, the high school on a college campus was able to reduce the dropout rate, improve attendance, and raise test scores.

CHAPTER 3

EQUALIZING OPPORTUNITY IN CALIFORNIA

Kenneth R. Weiss

Talk to higher education leaders in California and each one will say the same thing: One of their top worries is how to accommodate a "tidal wave" of students expected to flood through their campus gates in the next decade. So why, with the prospect of such a deluge, are California's public universities trying so hard to recruit even more students? Why did the University of California spend $147 million in the final academic year of the twentieth century to boost academic achievement in poor high schools so that more kids would be eligible for one of its eight undergraduate campuses? Why is the California State University system of 22 campuses sending thousands of students and faculty into the public schools to make sure more of their graduates will be prepared to handle university-level courses?

The reasons have less to do with pumping up the overall college population than with influencing whose faces will be reflected in the numbers. It has to do with California's undergoing a historic shift in its racial and ethnic makeup just as the state begins to grope its way into a post–affirmative action era. It's about what it means to be a public university that serves mostly White and Asian American students when Latinos and African Americans make up a majority of the state's schoolchildren. And all this, of course, boils down to a bottom line: Public institutions do what they must do to maintain the flow of goodwill from the citizenry and dollars from the legislature.

It doesn't take a Ph.D. in politics to figure this out. Listen to this rifle shot from Antonio Villaraigosa, speaker of the California State Assembly: "It is the university's job to open up to kids like me," Villaraigosa said. If the university doesn't make it happen, he said, "The legislature has to make sure UC is a place where our kids have an opportunity to attend." So the University of California and California State University are suddenly reaching deeper into public schools than ever before. Each of the two systems approaches the task differently, in keeping with its mission, self-interests, and the community it serves. Although bursting with ideas, neither university system has a grand plan of how to close the academic achievement gap among the races that produces the underrepresentation of minority students.

Instead, what has emerged are hundreds of experimental programs in an enthusiastic—sometimes frantic—effort to find a magical way to make their student bodies reflect the ethnic diversity of California's population. Plugging in anything that seems promising, universities now help elementary students learn to read. They push junior high students to take algebra. They guide high school students to get on track for college. They try to prepare the most promising minority students to compete for spots at the most elite universities. Much of the money pours into new programs, rather than expanding programs with a longer track record. Mary Catherine Swanson, who founded the successful Achievement Via Individual Determination (AVID) college-prep program in San Diego 20 years ago, complains about the poor coordination among all the newcomers flooding into the schools. "We are not unified and we trip over each other," she said. "The whole thing is topsy-turvy." The universities' most ambitious efforts attempt a top-to-bottom reform of a few designated schools. But mostly, these programs aim at boosting the chances of a select number of students. Narrowing the focus to only a few students troubles some education leaders, given how many others that strategy leaves behind.

"The problem in California is too big," said Patrick M. Callan, president of the National Center for Public Policy and Higher Education. "We have to figure out how to fix the schools, not reach into the schools and save a few kids from the schools they are in." But is that the role of the public university? Aside from improving the education of schoolteachers, is it reasonable to think universities, as outsiders, can swoop in and fix systemic problems that have been so resistant to internal reforms? Or is it good enough to help a few students and assuage guilt with the comfort that at least they're making an effort? It's too soon to say whether the universities are making much headway. Californians spent $38.1 billion in 1999–2000 on public schools. So what difference will a few million dollars or even a few hundred million dollars make? And how long will state legislators, whose attention spans and patience are shortened by voter-imposed term limits, be willing to sustain such funding when measurable gains in school improvement are so notoriously slow?

Student-Centered Programs

The efforts of California's universities to improve the public schools are only a small part of the educational landscape. The state adopted academically rigorous standards—insisting, for example, that textbooks, as well as teacher training, be linked to these standards. A high school exit exam is scheduled to come on line, as will new accountability measures ranking the schools by performance. But all these reforms are unlikely to change the mix of students who benefit. That's a potential niche for the universities.

Most of the disparate efforts to groom underprivileged students for college fall into one of two categories: Student-centered programs or those that deal with entire schools. Student-centered programs typically focus intensely on a small cadre of pupils, assembling tutors to improve their academic skills and mentors to spark dreams of a better life through higher education. The idea is that, though limited to a select few, such a concentrated effort will help these students quickly get up to speed and make them competitive for the best colleges. School-centered programs aim to improve inner-city or rural schools serving the poor—and thus the performance of their students. Typically, university educators often design the overall strategy and professors hold seminars to help teachers master their subjects. At places such as UCLA, professors rarely make it into the public schools, and so the campus hires veteran teachers as its envoys.

"Watch this," Sidnie Myrick tells the fourth-grade teacher. The din of the class has been rising with the heat, most students straying from their assignment of writing an in-class essay. Who could blame them? The hot Santa Ana winds have turned Room 28 at Stoner Elementary School in Los Angeles into an itchy, sweltering box that smells, well, like sweaty feet. A brown-haired girl, complaining about ants on her desk, drags her chair to another table, metal legs scraping the floor like fingers on a chalkboard. Two boys stab at each other with index fingers in an imaginary sword fight. So Myrick, a master teacher brought into Stoner Elementary by UCLA, pulls back from her quiet conference with the fourth-grade teacher and rises to her feet. Scanning the room of squirming 9-year-olds, she compliments one student for "nice work," then singles out the most rambunctious child: "Marta, do you need help with ideas?" The girl looks back startled, then sheepish. She shakes her head no. "Do you know what you are going to write next?" She nods. "When you're done, I want to read yours." Myrick scouts for other trouble-makers. All is quiet now. All 27 heads are down, pencils scratching on paper. "Great work, Room 28."

Myrick spends 2 days a week in elementary schools, hired by UCLA as a "literacy coach." She's much more than that. A former teacher with 12 years of classroom experience, she has become a mentor and confidant to the new teachers who churn through inner-city schools. She even hauled in a carpet-cleaning machine and shampooed a mildewed rug in a kindergarten class. "We try to be models for new teachers," Myrick said. "You do whatever you need to do, to make it more conducive for students to learn."

It's hard to coax UCLA professors into the gritty public schools, so the university has turned to hired help, like Myrick. Her rounds are part of a broad-scale effort to turn around 13 high schools—and their feeder schools—adopted by UCLA. Around the state, UC campuses have targeted 67 such high-school clusters, enrolling about 120,000 students. The goal is to undertake a long-term effort to revamp their entire academic culture. Jeannie L. Oakes, a UCLA education professor, explained that the idea is to replicate all the conditions that make it a natural act for students from upper-middle-class families to go to college.

First, UCLA officials push the schools to offer academically rigorous courses and prod teachers to develop a profound understanding of the subjects they teach. University representatives encourage parents to get personally involved—even become pushy—with the schools. They provide after-school programs to reinforce what students learn in the classroom and to mold their minds, so that students consider it normal to work hard and strive for college. UCLA also wants to recast its image among these students, so that the youngsters think of this big university as a place built for them, not somebody else. Only when that happens, Oakes said, can these inner-city students abandon the internal conflicts that may be holding them back. She said: "Then they can say, 'I don't have to act White. I don't have to cut off my connections to my family and neighborhood. UCLA is about me.'"

Is it working? As with just about every other aspect of the outreach program, the answer remains the same: It's too soon to tell. To be sure, there are encouraging signs. Parents are more engaged. Students talk more about college. Real strides may take years, though. Some suggest the results won't be fully realized for 13 years, the time it takes for a kindergarten class to matriculate through the twelfth-grade. UCLA has dozens of other strategies—designed for quicker results—in its patchwork quilt of outreach programs. The university hopes that some of the strategies will produce enough results to satisfy lawmakers angry over the 43% drop in African Americans admitted as freshmen to UCLA and the 33% decline in Latinos since California voters abolished affirmative action by passing Proposition 209. (UC Berkeley has seen even steeper declines in these minorities.)

The tricky part is that under revised admissions rules, which emphasize academic merit, the grades and test scores needed to make the cut at Berkeley and UCLA have soared. The average freshman at UCLA this year has a SAT score of 1,275 and grade-point average (GPA) of 4.13. (GPAs exceed

the 4-point scale because UC grants 5 points for an A in Advanced Placement or honors courses.) That makes minority recruitment an enormous
challenge for UCLA and Berkeley. They need to raise the test scores and grades
of Blacks and Latinos so, as one top administrator puts it, "they can drive
out some of the Whites and Asian-Americans." No one understands this better
than UCLA vice–chancellor Winston Churchill Doby. Out of his anger over
the loss of affirmative action has emerged the Career Based Outreach Program to boost the academic performance of students in some of the worst
schools in Los Angeles. It's an effort he leads with missionary zeal. On a
Saturday morning, Doby stands before 80 UCLA undergraduates, inspiring
them to rethink the limits of their potential and to carry the message of hard
work and determination into the high schools. He recounts his battle with
prostate cancer and how he committed himself to a top-notch workout to
speed his recovery. Then he linked up with a personal trainer who pushed
his exercise regime to a whole new level. "That's what this program is all
about. It's to stretch you to your maximum."

The Career Based Outreach Program absorbed the old "informational"
outreach at UCLA. Unlike the old program, which mostly informed students
about which college-prep courses and standardized tests they needed, this
pilot program has its own Japanese-model learning system: Let students first
wrestle with a problem and try to discover the answer for themselves. It has
its own philosophy cribbed from former UCLA basketball coach John
Wooden's Pyramid of Success: "Success is peace of mind, which is a direct
result of self-satisfaction in knowing you did your best to become the best
that you are capable of becoming."

What it lacks are enough UCLA students willing to become tutors, despite the allure of course credit and roughly $10-an-hour salaries. For now,
the program has only enough tutors to reach the top 80 or so freshmen, sophomores, and juniors at 19 low-performing high schools. Doby knows this is
just skimming the cream, but he stresses that UCLA has to make some headway somewhere—and fast. The legislature, which increased the UC system's
outreach budget by $38.5 million, wants to see results. UC officials hope the
legislature will be satisfied if they meet their own goal: a 100% increase in
minority students who meet UC's minimum eligibility requirements and a
50% increase in minorities with grades and test scores to compete for seats
at places like UCLA. "We have to build hope," Doby said, "by demonstrat-
ing [that] the best students in those low-performing schools can be competitive with students from any other school."

Still, such "creaming" undercuts the program's supply of undergraduates, who flock to other tutoring programs with more idealistic goals. "We
want to increase the academic achievement of all students, not just the cream
of the crop," said Cori Shepherd, who runs the African Student Union's tu-

toring program. She is disturbed by racial tracking. "In eighth grade, they decide who is going into algebra and who isn't. It isn't that the other students cannot do it, it's just that they get tagged and put into different classes. UCLA is coming in and reinforcing it." Oakes, the UCLA education professor, said she, too, is troubled by the selective approach of helping only a few students. She prefers the broader effort of working with UC partnership schools, which attempt to raise the achievement of all students in those schools. The problem here is scrounging up enough money to make a difference. Oakes calculates that UCLA spends about $40 a student at the partnership schools. That's the cost of about 2 hours of private tutoring. Such money gets quickly diluted, given all of the challenges.

Stoner Elementary isn't the worst school in the program; however, it offers a peek at what reformers face on the front lines. About 70% of its students have limited English skills, their standardized test scores lag far below average, and the entire student body is poor enough to qualify for free breakfast and lunch. Slightly more than 86% of the students are Latino (overwhelmingly of Mexican heritage), 7% are African American, and the remainder a smattering of different races.

Back in Room 28, fourth-grade teacher Dana Hasson gushes to Myrick about all the things she wants to try in her class. While her students write their essays, she and Myrick huddle over the phonics game and ways to divide the students into small groups so she can give a few pupils more individualized attention. "Now that you've done this, it's like, 'Duh!'" Hasson said. "They never show you this while student teaching." Myrick gives her a knowing smile. "It only took me 8 years to figure this out." Now it's time to push on to the next class. Myrick has another appointment on her rounds, and Hasson obviously doesn't want her to leave. "This helps so much," Hasson said, clutching her reworked lesson plan to her chest. "I wish I could give you something." She looks around her desk and comes up with a small offering. "How about a sticker?"

In the Classroom in Long Beach

About 30 miles south, Joe Potts, an English professor at California State University, Long Beach, guides seven students through a difficult passage of *The Odyssey*. These students are all freshmen—not in college, but in the ninth grade at Lakewood High School in Long Beach. "See how this word and this word fit together?" Potts asks a girl with long black hair and braces. "Doesn't that make sense?" At the table next to him, Keith Simms, a Cal State Long Beach senior, talks with another seven freshmen about how Odysseus prepares his sailors for the Sirens' call. "So what's he doing with the beeswax?"

Simms asks the group. "Making ear plugs?" offers a slender boy with a fashionable "bed-head" hairdo. It comes out as more of a question than a confident answer. Tufts of moussed hair point every which way. Simms congratulates him. The other students bend over their papers and jot down the answer.

With the Cal State professor and a pair of college-age tutors and two teachers, there are enough adults to break up all the kids into small groups to work on critical reading skills. The relationship hopes to boost the college-going rates of these students over the next 5 years. The programs reach about 10% of Lakewood High's 4,200 students. But instead of going for the cream, the focus is on students with grade-point averages of 2.0 to 2.9—the kind of kids who wouldn't make it to the university on their own. All students and their parents had to sign a contract to enter the special program. They agree to do their homework, attend class every day, and go to tutoring sessions after school whenever warranted.

The program is complemented by a larger systemic reform effort in Long Beach modeled after school–university collaborations around the country. Six years ago, Cal State Long Beach joined with the local community college and school district to form the Long Beach Education Partnership. The goal was to create "seamless education" from kindergarten through college, so that all children are prepared for higher education or the job market without needing remedial education or special preferences. The first step was a simple one: Get university faculty and public school teachers to talk to each other. Working with university faculty from math, English, and other departments, Long Beach schools adopted a set of rigorous academic standards. Now, they are close to aligning Long Beach high schools' exit exams with Cal State's entrance exams, so that if, for instance, a student demonstrates writing proficiency in the exit exam, that would satisfy the university's entrance requirement. Professors routinely visit schools to supervise student teachers, and teachers go to the Cal State campus to help prepare future teachers. Professors from many disciplines mix regularly with teachers to discuss everything from art to zoology at seminars, retreats, and conferences.

All this has impressed Kati Haycock, director of the Washington, D.C.–based Education Trust, which promotes K–16 collaborations around the country. Long Beach has managed to erode so many barriers, she said, "It's hard to know where one institution ends and the other one begins." The partnership also caught the attention of U.S. Education Secretary Richard W. Riley, who picked Cal State Long Beach as the site for his 1999 state-of-education address. "The Long Beach Education Partnership is a wonderful, wonderful example of all of the parts of American education fitting together," Riley said. "Seamless education really is the wave of the future."

To be sure, California State University campuses have always been deeply involved in the public schools, given the university's origin from a collection of teachers' colleges. Even after California adopted its master plan for higher education in 1960 and turned these colleges into the far-flung campuses of a state university, the campuses have kept much closer ties to public schools than have the campuses of the elite University of California. Cal State produces 60% of California's teachers, compared with the 4% who come out of the University of California. And Cal State enrolls twice as many undergraduates as UC, accepting anyone in the top third of his or her high school class, compared with UC's niche of the top 12.5%.

UC vs. Cal State

Thus it is that problems in academic preparation surface more readily on Cal State campuses. When Cal State officials tested all incoming freshmen last year, they discovered that 68% lacked the skills for college-level math or English. The figures were even more dismaying for Blacks and Latinos, forcing the vast majority into remedial classes. Five years ago, the Cal State Board of Trustees voted to abolish remedial classes and deny admission to students who weren't ready for college-level work. It was a hard-line stand for "the people's university," a place known for welcoming the sons and daughters of immigrants, ethnic minorities, and the first member of many families to attend college. Ultimately, the trustees backed down and decided to focus on helping high schools gradually reduce the number of students who need remedial courses to 10% of freshmen by 2007. "We must help those who are feeding us, namely kindergarten through twelfth grade," said trustee Ralph R. Pesquiera. "This is the most important thing we have to do."

As a consequence, all 22 Cal State campuses have plunged deeper into the public schools, focusing most intensely on the 232 high schools that send the university system the greatest number of students in need of remediation. Cal State Long Beach joined other campuses this year in offering math and English placement exams to students while they are juniors or seniors in high school. "If we can detect them early enough, I have found that the high schools are perfectly willing to help them get prepared for the university," said Robert C. Maxson, president of Cal State Long Beach. Maxson pointed out that fewer freshmen at his campus this year needed remedial classes than they did 5 years ago. Long Beach schools now retain a higher percentage of new teachers, and more students are taking and passing algebra. But test scores show mixed results, and other tangible improvement attributed to the partnership remains skimpy. Still, Cal State's chancellor, Charles B. Reed, said that the university had never worked harder at improving public schools. It's not an altruistic act. "If they get better," he said, "we get better."

Now, with their different approaches, the University of California and Cal State are seeking to do something even more difficult—to change the future of the young, to alter the course of their lives from what might otherwise have been in store for them. This is not simply an act of goodwill; the two universities have their own institutional interests as well. Cal State officials no longer blame the schools, given their role in preparing teachers. And UC officials no longer just cherry-pick the best students and forget about the remaining youngsters, those they might have ignored in years past. UC campuses are now deeply engaged with surrounding schools. This new attitude and the resulting changes in practice constitute, perhaps, the silver lining in the clouds that settled over the state of California after the political storm that ended affirmative action. The challenge for both systems as the new century begins will be persuading lawmakers to keep the dollars flowing while both universities sort out what really works. It will call for a tricky balancing act. The universities will have to show some immediate results, but at the same time must coax lawmakers into shifting dollars from fragmented pilot projects to long-term, school-based programs that will give students a chance to go to college several years down the line. It will be a time that tests the limits of just how much higher education is capable of accomplishing.

CHAPTER 4

MIDDLE COLLEGE HIGH SCHOOL IN MEMPHIS

Mickie Anderson

Joyce Mitchell has a hope chest filled with old notes and cards, dried-up flowers, and other souvenirs of life. She used to reach for one particular card on days when she needed an emotional lift. It said: "I regret picking up the paper this morning to see another article about your school, knowing the hard work you and all of your teachers do. One day you're going to get off this roller coaster." More recently, Mitchell, principal of Middle College High School on the campus of Shelby State Community College in Memphis, has rarely had to shuffle through her hope chest in search of that card. She doesn't need the boost anymore. Middle College High, by the end of the 1990s, was doing what the concept was designed to do: create tight bonds between teachers and students, foster collaboration between college and high school faculty members, and give students a first-hand feel for college even as they finish high school.

By its 13th year, the high school, which had such highs and lows that the "roller coaster" description was hardly an exaggeration, had settled onto a smoother, more comfortable track. "It's 100 . . . no, it's 1,000% better," Mitchell said. Middle College High at Shelby State was among the first replications of the middle college prototype launched in 1973 at LaGuardia Community College in the gritty Long Island City section of New York City's borough of Queens. There are now such programs around the country, each with the same goal: Target at-risk students believed to have college potential, plant them on a college campus, and get them headed toward higher education. The high school students have visible peer models in the college student body, attend small classes, and receive superior academic and support services. Some of the high school teachers teach in the college and the college professors, in the high school. The high school students are encouraged to take college courses and earn simultaneous high school and college credit. Some of the middle college programs have internship programs for students who earn credit for service work in the community.

On the national scene, the middle college high movement grew from its 1973 inception to 11 campuses in 1990 and to 25 campuses by 1999. The concept spread as school systems looked for ways to catch students, primarily minority and economically disadvantaged youngsters who so often disappear in large, urban school systems and who most desperately need a second chance. Despite the proliferation of the concept, Cecilia Cunningham, principal of the first middle college program at New York's LaGuardia Community College and a leader in the national movement, warned that the program cannot be replicated via blueprint—it must be tailored to each site. For example, her school targets students new to the United States, while in Las Vegas, the program reaches out to struggling sophomores. "The definition of kids who need middle college is different in every community," she said. Cunningham, who heads the consortium of middle college high programs, said the idea hasn't stopped growing. "There are always people interested in starting middle colleges," she said.

The program has thrived because an educational setting that lets disengaged students connect with teachers and administrators works, said Chery Wagonlander, principal at Mott Middle College High School on the campus of Mott Community College in Flint, Michigan. Wagonlander's doctoral dissertation focused on early graduates of Mott Middle College (MMC). She said that she thought that outcomes at other programs mirror those at Mott, although statistics from sites around the country are scarce. Her follow-up surveys of MMC graduates showed that between 64% to 74% of the school's graduates from 1994 to 1997 went on to college. Almost two-thirds of the members of those high school graduating classes attended Mott Community College, which illustrates the impact that the approach can have on the pipeline leading into the host institution.

The story of Middle College High in Memphis is one of conflict and collaboration. It is also about perseverance. The program's start-up was on the fast track from the outset; the early years were a roller coaster of wild loops and hairpin turns. Raymond Bowen, then the president of Shelby State, and Willie Herenton, then the school superintendent, agreed in 1986 to try to secure the funds for a middle college program in Memphis. The Ford Foundation had a pot of money waiting to be snapped up by school systems willing to try the idea. Bowen and Herenton clearly wanted to act fast to get a share for Memphis. In their haste, though, they seemed to forget to discuss with Shelby State's faculty the changes that would soon take place on the campus. Shelby State faculty members said they were given little—some say no—advance warning of the middle college high program and scant explanation of how it would work. The early days, with no information and some misinformation, were nearly disastrous to Middle College High.

One of the early problems was a shortage of funds despite the $276,000 in seed money from the Ford Foundation and another $50,000 pledged by local businesses. Herenton, the school superintendent, ran into a tough budget fight in the summer of 1990. His school system faced cuts after both city and county governments refused to fund the schools at the level school officials said they needed. Herenton looked at the fledgling Middle College High School and saw the $740,000 savings that shutting down the school would bring. But he apparently did not recognize how strongly students, parents, and teachers felt about the 3-year-old program. The city school board, acting on Herenton's request, voted to drop the program. A week later, in an outpouring of emotion, students and parents pleaded for the program to be saved. Students crowded the school board auditorium to tell the elected board that the school had prevented them from becoming dropouts or unemployment statistics.

"This is my second chance, this is everybody's second chance," a student, April Gray, told the board, tears welling. "This is it. Give us our school back." Dan Townsend, a social worker at a local children's center, told board members he had seen first-hand the difference the school had made: "They've been given a second chance . . . to believe in themselves, perhaps for the first time in their lives." Unable to resist the emotional pleas, board members voted to retain the school. Middle College High would survive.

Joyce Mitchell, who had never been a principal before winning the job as Middle College's first principal, was overjoyed. She interpreted the students' emotionally favorable response as validation that the program was working. Just a day after the program's rescue by the school board, however, there was an uproar that left Mitchell wondering why she had ever wanted the job. The July 4 edition of *The Commercial Appeal*, the local daily newspaper, carried a follow-up story to the previous day's news of the program's survival. Unlike the students and teachers at Middle College High, Shelby State's faculty members, it said, were not at all happy at the turn of events.

The news took many by surprise, although it probably shouldn't have. The discontent over inadequate consultation, which had been an undercurrent from the start, had bubbled to the surface. When it looked in June 1990 as if the program were doomed, Professor Don Reaves told the newspaper: "There was great joy, dancing in the hallways." Another professor, Jim Williams, a biology teacher, said of the high school, "We were so happy. It felt so good to finally be rid of it." Members of the college's faculty told stories of being threatened and shoved by the high school students. They said they had filed formal complaints with Shelby State administrators about students' being vulgar and unruly but that their concerns had been discounted. Then the critics took aim and unloaded the phrase that still stings. "Hoodlum High," they called it.

Shelby State's enrollment at the time was 3,000. Middle College High was growing, and the challenge of providing enough space for both institutions was becoming an issue. The high school and the community college were vying for the limited amount of room available in the college facilities. College classes were being squeezed into ever-tighter spaces. Faculty members worked split schedules because of the space crunch, forced to offer fewer classes and even turning away students. Annoyed faculty members spent their mornings circling the parking lots for spaces, having to compete with high school as well as college students. Irritated at losing their space and not being let in on the program from the beginning, Shelby State faculty members had little patience when confronted with high school students who yelled in the halls or made silly faces in the windows to college classrooms. Angry professors lashed out in the newspaper article.

Putting An End to Anti–High School Feelings

Mitchell, who guided Middle College High through those rough times, said that if she had known what the early years would have in store, she might not have even applied for the job. "I mean, when I think about it, I was totally unprepared," she said. In truth, the conflict between the Middle College High students and the community college faculty might just as likely have been fueled by longstanding friction between Shelby State faculty and administrators of the college itself. Since the college's leadership turned over several times during the early 1990s, discord would probably have become the norm even if the high school had not been created . "They were the toughest ones," Cunningham said of the college's faculty. "There are some institutions where the voices of dissatisfaction and dissent are allowed to be out loud. And this was one of those places."

Controversy continued at Shelby State even as the high school settled in. Bud Amann, the college's president, was often the target of brickbats after his arrival in the late 1990s at what ultimately grew to be a 4,000-student campus. "The faculty always felt that it had been pushed upon them," Steve Haley, the former faculty president, said of the high school in 1999. But Amann tried to shift the dissatisfaction away from the high school. Familiar with the middle college concept from his days as a community college administrator in New York, he gave Middle College High critics no room to protest when, right out of the gate, he professed strong support for the program. He was steadfast in his support for the high school. The family atmosphere at the high school was something the college would do well to emulate, he often told Shelby State's faculty. In addition, members of the college faculty came to recognize that having the high school on campus helped bring more potential students into the Shelby State fold, a not inconsiderable advantage in light of the enrollment problems that plagued the college in the 1990s.

Another factor easing the conflict between the college and the high school was Mitchell's repeated advice to her faculty to go about their work and ignore the distractions. LaGuardia's Cunningham said that there was little the Middle College High principal or faculty could do about problematic leadership at their host college other than to hang on and weather the storm. But, she said, when all else fails, longevity helps. "Time changes things," she said. "They are now very much a part of that college culture. The longer you're there, the more that happens." Educators on both sides say that these are some of the lessons about collaboration that they have learned:

• The faculty of the host school must be brought in during the planning stage so that they understand the intent of the program and have time to discuss potential problems. If the college faculty isn't behind the concept, it won't fly.

• The program must be sold realistically. Mitchell came to believe that it was a mistake to market Middle College High as a dropout-prevention program. To her, the term "dropout prevention" conveyed optimism and hope; but she acknowledged that critics thought the worst of the school's students when they heard the term.

• There are differences of opinion about the advisability of spreading high school students across the college campus. Some believe that the younger students should be physically integrated into the campus, but others think this approach just adds to the difficulties and that problems can be avoided by segregating the high schoolers.

• Politically, it is smart for the high school to maintain a strong relationship with the college administration. If there is turnover at the top, the high school should strive for a seat on the presidential search committee—or at least make sure that members of the high school faculty are a visible part of the welcoming committees for new top administrators. Serving on collegewide committees is wise for the same reason. The better acquainted college faculty are with their Middle College High counterparts, the more likely they'll be to support the program.

Progress at the High School

Mitchell said one lesson she learned the hard way was to meet controversy head-on. At first, she and the Middle College High teachers knew no other tactic than to turn the other cheek to their critics and refuse to be baited into a sniping contest with Shelby State faculty members. To keep peace, for instance, principal Mitchell fussed at students over every peep, an approach that she later reflected upon with some embarrassment. "I would just jump at the slightest noise. You would have thought I was the Energizer bunny or something," she said, recalling how she tried to prevent high schoolers from incurring the wrath of the college faculty. "But then one of the teachers came in and said, 'You really need to chill a little bit.'"

Even as the relationship between the high school and the college improved, old animosities had lingering effects. If the air-conditioning broke down in the high school section the building, for instance, students in the high school wondered if it was a deliberate act on the part of college officials who didn't like them. And if a high school teacher saw a cafeteria worker gazing at a table left in disarray, she scurried over to make sure the worker knew it was not a high school student who had left the mess.

Mitchell grew to be a more savvy administrator, learning to collect statistics on campus incidents she felt were wrongly blamed on Middle College High students. For instance, if a fire alarm sounded, Mitchell picked up the phone and asked the fire marshal what had happened so that she would be prepared when someone pointed a finger at one of her students. She also learned to keep better track of incidents on campus so that she could demonstrate that her students were not the only ones involved in the occasional scrap or loud argument. The Middle College High teachers made a logistical decision that helped quiet the critics—and their students. After much wrangling, they developed an idea for placing the high school on the same class schedule as the college, putting an end to complaints by college faculty members about high schoolers' noise in the halls during college class time. High school students now have 60-minute classes 3 days a week and 90-minute classes 2 days a week, replicating the schedule of the college.

By the start of 2000, Middle College High was enjoying greater tranquility. Even among students who usually eschewed all fashions except the urban staples of Nautica, Hilfiger, and Fubu, there was enough school spirit that they cheerfully wore Shelby State hats or T-shirts. Students who graduated and went to local colleges came back frequently just to hang around in the office and catch up with friends and teachers. On the day in 1999 when the high school's new yearbooks arrived at the building, students huddled around Mitchell's desk, pointing to their pictures on the pages and reminiscing with obvious fondness. The tranquil scene attested to the high school's progress from the days of constant conflict, underscoring the fact that Mitchell and her staff finally were able to teach without the need to combat continual distractions.

Teachers increasingly found that not having to deal with constant conflict meant they could focus on the collaborative projects that Middle College High is all about. Some teachers have served as adjunct faculty at the college, while other teachers have turned to college professors for help in preparing students for the state's standardized test. Also in the works was a plan to enlist college faculty members to help create a more seamless curriculum between the last year of high school and the first year of college.

But how has the high school worked academically, which, after all, is the ultimate rationale for forming middle college high schools? The data are encouraging. Students drop out at a lower rate compared with overall dropout rates in Memphis, attendance is better, and test scores have gone up in recent years, including dramatic improvements in writing scores that mirrored the district's improvements. In keeping with citywide improvements in writing, the scores of Middle College High students climbed for 2 straight years in the late 1990s. Tennessee students take a writing test that is graded on a scale of 0 to 6. A score of 4 or higher is considered proficient; 63% of the Middle College High students reached that mark in 1999, compared with 48% in 1998 and 33% in 1997.

The school trimmed its dropout rate to 3.4% a year, well below the 8.5% annual rate that continued to plague the city school district. The school's daily attendance rate, at 93.4%, was much better than the district's average of 88.6% daily attendance for high school students. One sign of the improved climate was that some of the most strident critics of the high school from the Shelby State faculty eventually enrolled their children in the high school program.

Good news, of course, is sometimes tempered by less encouraging reports about areas that need work. Raising scores on the American College Test (ACT) was among the goals outlined in the annual school improvement plan required by the city school district. High school students at Middle College High scored an average of 15.7 on the college entrance test, compared with the district's average score of 17.1. The highest possible score on the ACT is 36.

Middle College High is given room to teach, as teachers put it, although in 1998, despite having its hands full with its unique curriculum and format, the school had to fall into lockstep with the district's other 160 schools and choose a redesign model. The staff chose Expeditionary Learning/ Outward Bound, a model most often used by elementary schools, but one the Middle College High teachers felt was a good fit with the way they like to teach. The expeditionary learning concept was in evidence during the first week of school in 1999, as teachers set up indoor and outdoor stations. When students arrived, they were confronted with different types of bewildering situations—such as a librarian who refused to speak to them in English or a Muslim school administrator who insisted that the entire group pray to Allah until the students protested that they were Christian and such prayers betrayed their own religion. The exercise was not only meant to help the new students get to know each other, but also to help set the stage for a school year in which students think about others' feelings before acting.

For former student Nicole Gray, though, none of the pedagogy mattered, except for the tenet of Middle College High's philosophy that says every teacher will be not just a teacher but also a "teacher/counselor." There were cases in which teachers had to take homeless students to shelters. They've sat in court, for moral support more than anything else, when an 18-year-old student sought and won custody of her younger sister because their mother was on drugs. Not all Middle College High School students faced such trauma, but most, like Gray, were considered at-risk. When she entered Middle College High, Gray was a world away from reaching her potential. Much of her time outside class was spent hanging out with friends and goofing off. Yet she had career aspirations. "When I was in the ninth grade, I wanted to be a data processor," she said. "I had looked through some vo-tech books and I thought, 'Well, I type really well. This is something.'" She and three of her girlfriends responded to the pitch when a Middle College High representative came to their school to explain the program, though they wavered in their commitment before finally signing up.

Once in Middle College High, Gray enrolled in a college-level art appreciation class, but she didn't tell the professor she was still a 16-year-old high school student. She earned an A. She took other classes and did just fine in them, too. With encouragement from Mitchell, who often took her to McDonald's for after-school french fries and chats about the future, Gray began to think she might actually be able to get through college. Gray graduated from the University of Tennessee's law school in 1998 and now has a fellowship, handling litigation work for the American Civil Liberties Union that focuses on improving relations between African Americans and the police. She lives on Maryland's eastern shore, an area she loves, and every day, she goes to work happy.

If someone had told Gray when she was 15 that she would become a practicing attorney, she'd have buckled with laughter. She imagined what would have happened if she had stayed at her old school. "I think I would've been a data processor. I really do," she said. "I think I would have gotten a job where I was paid for what I did, instead of what I knew." And that, Shelby State president Amann says, is precisely why more colleges and high schools should try collaborative efforts such as the Middle College High program. "It's easy for me to preach on about it," he said. "It's taking students who otherwise would be lost to our society and helping them become productive citizens. What's not to like about that?"

CHAPTER 5

THE EL PASO COLLABORATIVE FOR ACADEMIC ACHIEVEMENT

Duchesne Paul Drew

In the summer of 1992, teachers and principals in the El Paso area gathered for a professional development program that forced them to look deep inside themselves and ask some tough questions. *Did they really believe all children could learn at high levels or just some? Were the schools they taught in good enough for their children? Were they willing to take greater responsibility for their students' learning?*

With those questions came an offer to help schools in that corner of Texas that were willing to try some new approaches. In the years after 1992, the El Paso Collaborative for Academic Excellence built a communitywide network that helped transform the philosophical and structural foundations of the city's schools. The Collaborative's driving force has been a commitment to ensuring the academic success of all students—from kindergarten through the university level.

El Paso's three independent school districts—El Paso, Socorro, and Ysleta—didn't have much to brag about in the early 1990s. While a handful of students excelled, too many failed to acquire the skills that they would need to be productive, successful adults. The Collaborative attacked El Paso's chronic low achievement on several fronts. It helped establish a standards-based curriculum and the corresponding instruction that schools could adapt to their particular buildings. It helped restructure both the professional development training for existing teachers as well as the teacher preparation for education majors at the University of Texas at El Paso (UTEP). It helped build the capacity of principals and other school administrators to lead and

---

sustain education reform efforts in their buildings. And the Collaborative engaged parents and community leaders in shaping and supporting the reform efforts. All of these initiatives took place in a county where 42% of the school-age children live below the federal poverty level.

The timing of the hard-hitting questions that El Paso educators asked themselves in 1992 was perfect for Triana Olivas, who was still settling in as principal of Sageland Elementary in the Ysleta Independent School District. As a new administrator, Olivas was hungry for the guidance and resources the Collaborative could provide. The low expectations and low energy level at Sageland reminded her too much of the elementary school she had attended as a youngster in El Paso. Olivas wanted to change Sageland into a place that was child-centered and exciting, but she needed help.

The Collaborative's staff, taking such steps as bringing in speakers and handing out articles on the latest research findings, exposed Olivas and scores of educators across the city to the ideas that might transform their schools. The Collaborative did not impose or prescribe a single model for school reform; it built the capacity of principals, teachers, and parents to re-create their buildings in the images they envisioned. The training taught Olivas how to be a reflective leader, a principal who could see her own strengths and weaknesses reflected in the successes and failures of her students and teachers. Similarly, she said, her teachers learned to assess their own performance based on how their students did. The more Olivas learned through the Collaborative, the more she had available to share with her staff.

Although the teachers initially committed themselves to reform, Olivas encountered resistance once she actually began to try to make changes. From adopting new curriculum materials to switching classroom assignments, Sageland teachers had to make a lot of adjustments. Olivas's darkest day came when test scores came back that first spring and students' passing rates on the Texas Assessment of Academic Skills (TAAS), the state's chief barometer of school performance, had dropped. After all their risk taking and hard work, the school was just 2 points above being labeled low-performing, the state's lowest rating. It was a tough blow, but an outcome they knew was possible because reform efforts don't always pay off in measurable ways during the first year.

The meeting at which Olivas shared the disappointing results with her staff was a turning point for the school. "I took a deep breath and I prayed a lot before I met with them," she said. After breaking the news, Olivas figuratively opened the door. "You can either join me in continuing the journey, or I will do whatever I can if any of you want to leave now," she told them. Instead of a mass exodus, Olivas got a renewed commitment to go forward. And it paid off. From 1994 to 1998 the percentage of students passing the reading, writing and math TAAS tests in the school rose from 53.9% to 86.8%—a 32.9 percentage-point jump. Quite an accomplishment for a school where a host of social difficulties were associated with the almost nine out of ten students who qualified for subsidized lunches. Even more impressive was the replication of Sageland's growth rate across the district, which saw a 32.5 percentage-point increase in the number of elementary students passing all three tests. Today, Sageland, a 1999 Blue Ribbon School, is a place where teachers have grown to expect more of themselves and their students. Sageland has become a school where teachers confidently enroll their own children.

The 7-year journey took its toll on some staff members. About one-third of Olivas's staff left because Sageland was no longer a place where they wanted to work. Olivas had no trouble attracting good teachers to replace them. For Terri Arias, a 13-year veteran in her first year at Sageland, moving to the school forced her to step back and look more closely at how she was teaching. Although her former school was a good one, with high expectations for its students, Arias said Sageland has a different rhythm. "It's really opened up my creative spirit that I had my first year of teaching. It's made me open my eyes again to the way I was teaching." As she spoke, Arias's fifth-graders sat quietly, cutting letters out of newspapers so they could build their spelling words. Ongoing assessment of what works, what doesn't, and why is woven into the fabric of Sageland. In addition to weekly staff meetings, Olivas has a rotation, meeting with teachers, by grade level, for a half-day of reflection every 6 weeks. "It's exhausting, but you never lose sight of why [you're doing it], and you're always looking to move to the next level," Olivas said. "That's just been the mode from the very beginning."

What Made It Work

The Collaborative worked in El Paso for the following reasons:

- People in that relatively self-contained community saw an educational and economic crisis in their midst and recognized their shared interest in addressing it.
- Leaders in the city were committed to real change and were willing to work cooperatively.
- Texas's expanding accountability system created incentives for K–12 and university reforms.
- The Pew Foundation and National Science Foundation provided early and sustained financial support so that new initiatives would have time to take hold.

• The Collaborative focused on simultaneous development of standards, teachers, principals, and academic programs.

The right mix of fear, hope, and fortune led to the Collaborative's creation. When Susana Navarro moved back to El Paso, her hometown, from southern California in 1991, she knew she wanted to continue working to improve children's education. But she didn't know how. Navarro, a 1968 UTEP graduate and Stanford Ph.D., had devoted years to civil rights and education issues, most recently for California's Achievement Council. Navarro laid the groundwork for what became the Collaborative by talking to local people about their hopes and dreams for the city. "There was great interest in trying something new, there was a willingness here," she recalled. Navarro found a kindred spirit in Diana Natalicio, UTEP's president. El Paso finds advantages and disadvantages in being an isolated community. The university draws 85% of its students from El Paso County and prepares about 60% of the schoolteachers in the area. "There was kind of that recognition that we were a closed loop, that we are in fact a single community, and that if the problem was going to be addressed, we were the ones who were going to have to address it," Natalicio recalled. "Once you get there, then it's a question of pulling together the partners, and that's how the Collaborative got rolling.

Like its diverse programs and partners, the Collaborative's funding comes from a variety of sources. Its annual budget in real dollars is about $4.5 million. That figure climbs to about $11 million once shared costs and in-kind donations are included, according to Navarro. The Collaborative got off the ground thanks to donated space and funding from the university as well as a small planning grant from the Pew Charitable Trusts. Grants from Coca-Cola and the National Science Foundation, as well as money from the school districts, rounded out the original funding. In subsequent years, the Collaborative's budget grew with more substantial and continuing support from Pew, the state of Texas, and the U.S. Department of Education, among others.

One block east of Sageland Elementary sits Bel Air High School, another campus embarked on a journey of educational transformation. When principal Vernon Butler assumed his post in the fall of 1995, he encountered a staff that he thought was content with mediocrity. "We needed teachers that would believe in students, regardless of where they were," he said. Superintendent Anthony Trujillo, halfway through the year, announced that everyone at the school, with the exception of Butler, would have to reapply for his or her position. The reconstitution gave Butler the freedom to start over with a team of people who looked in the eyes of their students and saw potential. About half of the school's 130 professional staff members were retained. The rest transferred to other schools or retired. Butler filled vacancies by hiring freshly minted teachers. Most were recent UTEP graduates, and a number were second-career professionals who were working toward alternative certification. They were green, but they possessed a key quality. "They had no preconceived notions of students and what their abilities and disabilities were," according to Susana Gonzalez, Bel Air's dean of instruction.

The marriage of new teachers and experienced instructors led to great discussions among faculty members. The neophytes brought a sense of real-world expectations, while the more seasoned educators knew best how to translate those standards into classroom instruction. With the Collaborative's help, Bel Air and a dozen other area high schools won funding from the National Science Foundation's Urban Systemic Initiatives. The Initiative supported reform efforts in math and science instruction across the country. The additional funding allowed the 13 area high schools to adopt a new integrated math curriculum called SIMMS-IM (Systemic Initiative for Montana Integrated Mathematics and Science-Integrated Mathematics). Little by little the SIMMS classes took over Bel Air's math department. The school, which was named a Texas Blue Ribbon School in the fall of 1999, also reshaped its language arts programs.

The View from the University

Arturo Pacheco, dean of the College of Education at UTEP, can scan the factories and shanties of Juarez, Mexico, through the windows of his office. The *maquiladoras* and *colonias*, as they are called, are a constant reminder of the depth of need just beyond the campus. When the Collaborative was created, the initial focus was on reforming K–12 schools and improving the skills and resources of the teachers already working in those buildings. But stopping there would have been like trying to bail water out of a sinking boat without plugging a gaping hole. So the university and the school systems committed themselves to simultaneous renewal. "We can't start preparing new kinds of teachers and send them to old-fashioned schools," Pacheco said. "These reforms have to go hand in hand."

But all the keys to improving the preparation of education majors weren't in the hands of Pacheco and his faculty. In fact, 80% of the coursework education majors take is taught in the university's colleges of liberal arts and sciences. So Pacheco, with Natalicio's help, began a broader conversation among the College of Education faculty, the liberal arts and science faculty, and public school leaders. "Starting and maintaining the conversation was perhaps the most important thing we did. Because you can't mandate these things, you don't start top down," Pacheco said. They cultivated relationships by hosting a series of year-long institutes about general education issues and invited 25 to 30 key university leaders and public school officials to participate. Deans, principals, department chairs, professors, and district administrators turned out to explore broad educational topics, such as "What's an educated person?" and "What's the role of schooling in a democracy?"

The regular meetings provided a forum for K–12 and university educators to develop links. In part, this was built on mutual griping. It gave principals a chance to vent about the shortcomings of the teachers UTEP was turning out, and it allowed the university faculty to express their dissatisfaction with the caliber of students the local school districts were producing. After the air cleared, participants set about devising solutions to their common problems. One of the primary concerns that arose during the discussions was that students at the university weren't spending enough time in schools before they graduated. So Pacheco and his faculty scrapped the traditional program that required education majors to wait until their last semester of college to enter a classroom setting. It was replaced by a program that resembles the medical school model, in which pre-service teachers spend most of their senior year as interns in schools working alongside experienced teachers. Also, seniors were split into small groups to pursue their core classes and internships together, fostering supportive relationships within their groups. UTEP's education majors ended up spending 750 hours working with mentor teachers in public schools during their last two semesters.

The transition to the new, field-based model wasn't easy. It required condensing some education courses to create more time for in-school training. Because UTEP is a commuter campus and most students work, the new system also played havoc with students' schedules. "People were saying, 'But I ought to be able to become a teacher by taking night classes,'" Pacheco observed. "It's like becoming a doctor without ever having seen patients."

Another central element in the revamping of teacher preparation was the effort to deepen the future teachers' understanding of and connection to the families and communities the schools served. The feedback the university got from parents and community activists led school officials to adjust the curriculum to include coursework and field components focusing on the community and working with parents. "We're trying to produce teachers who are not going to walk into the classroom and lock the door and think 'This is my world,'" Pacheco said. In addition, the school now requires all its students to complete at least the equivalent of 2 years of Spanish. About two-thirds of Pacheco's students come from homes where adults speak Spanish, but many of the youngsters don't know the language. By the time they graduate, all the students—regardless of whether their surname is Garcia or Green—are expected to be able to speak Spanish well enough to welcome a parent into their classroom and get the relationship going.

All of the Collaborative's members were key to its success, but UTEP's contribution to the effort was truly essential. The university provided much of the physical space, expertise, and other resources necessary for teachers and principals to examine their practices. It also took great steps to look inward and improve the quality of its teacher preparation program. Moreover, Natalicio's stature in the community at large helped win broad support for the Collaborative. Her personal devotion to its mission—she only missed two board meetings in the first 8 years—set an important standard of commitment.

The state's efforts to raise standards extended to the colleges and universities that prepare teachers. Every September, university presidents across Texas get a letter from the state telling them how their graduates performed on the teacher certification test and whether their school keeps its accreditation. Unless at least 75% of all students, as well as 75% of students in each subgroup (e.g., black students or Hispanic students), pass, the university risks losing its right to prepare future teachers. As it does on the K–12 level, the state's accountability system requires universities to take responsibility for the success of students in all subgroups. Institutions of higher education can't mask poor performance by a subgroup by averaging the passing rates for all their students. "No single entity can raise the overall achievement of all the kids in El Paso," Pacheco said. "The future of this community depends on the achievement of all the kids. We think we're on the right track, but we also know how much more there is to do."

Another key partner in the Collaborative was the El Paso Interreligious Sponsoring Organization (EPISO), a community organizing group that made sure parents have a voice in local school reform efforts. In a city with many poor and uneducated adults, it's easy for educators to overlook or limit parental involvement. And parents in such communities often need to be prodded to participate in school activities because they don't always see what role they can play in helping schools improve. EPISO, part of the Industrial Areas Foundation, a social and political action group, works to bridge the gaps between schools and families. Ysleta Elementary is one of EPISO's—and the Collaborative's—biggest success stories. It is a school where 90% of the children qualify for federally subsidized lunch and half the students are in bilingual programs. It's also a school that blossomed because it was willing to make parents partners in its transformation.

The first concrete change began with a simple gesture, inviting parents into the building. The invitation surprised Petra Porras, who walked her grandchildren to school everyday. Years earlier, when Porras's children attended Ysleta Elementary, parents were not allowed beyond the front door, where they dropped their children off or picked them up. The invisible barrier at the front door was burned into Porras's memory, so much so that it took the school's parent educator several attempts to coax her into the building.

Once she stepped inside, Porras discovered her presence and ideas could make a difference not just for her grandchildren, but for all the students at Ysleta Elementary. "It was wonderful to know that there was a role for me, that there was something I could do," Porras said. Although she started by ironing graduation gowns, Porras soon found herself on a traffic safety committee. She and other parents who initially spent their volunteer time making copies and cutting out letters for bulletin boards eventually graduated to working on more important things, like an extensive after-school program and a new school building. Students have good reason to stick around when the school day ends at Ysleta Elementary. They can study music, play chess, create works of art, or learn ballet folklorico with community members in their brand-new, high-tech building.

Although teachers in the building were not initially welcoming, the parents' initiative commanded respect, especially because students' excitement about the extracurricular activities spilled over into the regular school day. Over time, the tensions eased. Teachers even came to rely on some parents to serve as motivational speakers who could encourage students to work hard in school by telling of their back-breaking years cleaning bathrooms and picking fruit because they didn't have an education. EPISO taught parents how to advocate for their children. They also learned how to help their children be more successful in school. "We look at ourselves as a learning community, all of us," principal Dolores DeAvila said. While the partnership with EPISO took hold and bore fruit at Ysleta Elementary, not all schools were as successful in working with the organization. The community group's approach required schools to share more decision-making power than some principals and teachers wished to do.

All three districts—El Paso, Socorro, and Ysleta—changed superintendents after 1992, being part of an administrative merry-go-round not unusual in urban schools. But the Collaborative was a source of consistency through the transitions. A wide range of community leaders sit on the Collaborative's board: Navarro, Natalicio, each of the three districts' superintendents, the president of El Paso Community College, the executive director of the regional education service center, EPISO's lead organizer, the president of the Greater El Paso Chamber of Commerce, the president of the El Paso Hispanic Chamber of Commerce, the mayor, and a county judge.

Sustaining the Collaborative has been a continuous challenge to motivate and move a complex system with partners and situations that no single entity controls. "It makes you want to cry tears of joy. And it makes you want to pull your hair out," said Navarro, who regularly hosts educators and journalists interested in learning about the Collaborative. By definition, it was still a work in progress at the end of the 1990s. But in many respects, Natalicio said, the biggest challenge remains the same. "I think the hardest thing is helping people change their attitudes and expectations of all the young people that they work with, whether they're at kindergarten, ninth grade or the university. The greatest challenge is to get people to believe there is talent everywhere. . . . And that the real responsibility for educators is to create opportunities for that talent to flourish."

PART III

Standards

Expectations have much to do, of course, with academic success. In the first place, if elementary and secondary schools do not expect enough from their students, many of those youngsters will end up with high school diplomas that signify little or they may not graduate at all. Second, many of those who want to continue their education will be ill equipped for postsecondary studies.

During the 1990s, standards were raised and students in many locales were expected to complete a more demanding program in order to complete high school and qualify for college. Moreover, statewide examinations were instituted in some places so that students could demonstrate achievement, although controversy frequently swirled around these tests. Some states chose to deal with the issue of standards by setting out to do more to unify standards from elementary schools through secondary schools through colleges so that curriculum and expectations could be aligned.

One such state was Maryland, which sought to unify education with its Partnership for Teaching and Learning, K–16 program. This approach aimed to raise standards, thereby making it more likely that students going on to higher education would be equipped for the challenge. Maryland made progress even though its K–16 partnership was informal, had little operating authority, and had no operating budget. The fragility of the approach could be seen in the fact that it depended very much on goodwill among the three ranking executives—the state university chancellor, the state schools superintendent, and the higher education secretary—who launched the effort. Mike Bowler found indications of success in Maryland and was able to garner policy implications that could be of use to other states.

Oregon spent much of the last decade trying to build its own approach, Proficiency-Based Admissions Standards System, usually called PASS, to create what it hoped would be a seamless connection between precollegiate schools and higher education. High school students would demonstrate mastery of performance standards to gain admission to Oregon's 7 universities and 17 community colleges. By the end of the 1990s, according to William Graves, there were signs that the educational systems of schools and institutions of higher education were growing more integrated and teachers were drawing more quality work from their students.

In Georgia, as Ernie Suggs describes it in Chapter 8, the state worked at different educational levels to improve a system in which many students were lagging seriously behind national norms. The P–16 Initiative—the P stressing the important role of prekindergarten education—created 15 regional councils around Georgia to advise school districts in the setting of standards. Looming throughout these deliberations was the University System of Georgia's Board of Regents. "Once we got into it, it was clear that the partnerships needed to be broader, and the chancellor hired me to strengthen the university's partnerships," said Jan Kettlewell, who sat at the helm of the statewide P–16 Council.

CHAPTER 6

MARYLAND'S K–16 PARTNERSHIP

Mike Bowler

Robert Rice couldn't believe his eyes. A meeting of Maryland mathematics educators—high school teachers and college professors—erupted in shouting, crying, and, as participants stomped from the room, the tipping of chairs. Why such behavior? Was this a meeting to discuss promotions or parking privileges? No, it was a failed attempt to agree on the "core learning goals" of high school algebra.

For much of the century, these two groups from both sides of the academic divide had had little to do with each other. But here they were, the collegiate and precollegiate educators, struggling over a crucial question: What should high school students know about mathematics—or English, or science, or any of the other core subjects? Rice, an assistant superintendent in the state education department, was observing an exercise in connection with Maryland's Partnership for Teaching and Learning, K–16, a cumbersome name for an effort to bridge the historic gap between precollegiate and higher education by raising standards up and down the academic line.

Formed in 1995 by the heads of the state's three education segments, the Partnership sought to move Maryland toward an education system in which a high school diploma guarantees admission to college or a good job and in which schoolteachers and university professors are in accord on what should be taught—and when. It hasn't been easy. There's a long history of misunderstanding and miscommunication between collegiate and precollegiate educators, between employers and the schools that train their workers, and between education professors and their colleagues in arts and sciences. There have been mistakes and delays. The K–16 Partnership is an informal one with little operating authority and no operating budget. But Maryland has jumped out ahead of many states and has lessons to offer them.

The K–16 architects were the state university chancellor, Donald N. Langenberg; the state schools superintendent, Nancy S. Grasmick; and the higher education secretary, Patricia S. Florestano. In 1995, the three, at the suggestion of Langenberg, determined to put aside turf protection and create a single education system for Maryland, seamless as a bridal veil. Aided by grants from the Pew Charitable Trusts, the three Maryland officials marshaled forces to raise academic standards, reform teacher education, and guarantee equal educational opportunity in all Maryland schools. Each of those goals was fraught with problems and challenges.

Standards setting wasn't new to Maryland. In 1993, after years of discussion, the state launched the Maryland School Performance Assessment Program (MSPAP), testing students in grades 3, 5, and 8 and using the results to judge the performance of schools. High-performing schools get cash awards, and failures are put on a "reconstitution-eligible" list. Maryland developed its own test because officials felt nationally normed commercial tests were not challenging enough, nor did they adequately measure student performance. But Maryland, like the governors who established "Goals 2000" in 1989, may have set its sights too high. The goal was to have 70% of the students scoring at the satisfactory level by 2000. By 1999, though, more than half had not passed the demanding tests, average scores statewide had actually declined slightly between 1998 and 1999, and 97 schools (83 of them in Baltimore City) were on the reconstitution list.

MSPAP profoundly changed the culture of education in Maryland, some say for the worse. Principals and teachers came under heavy pressure to raise scores in the annual tests, given in May. They will promise to kiss pigs or roll in the mud if that's what it takes to accomplish that goal. "We're totally Mizpapped," said Edna Greer, principal of Leith Walk Elementary School in Baltimore, employing an acronym that's in the lexicon of Marylanders from the ski slopes of Appalachia to the crab shanties of the eastern shore. Greer's school, the largest elementary in the state with 1,100 students, embodied her words. Everyone was attuned to the battery of performance-based tests, which require students to observe, analyze, make graphs, predict, and generally use "higher-order" thinking skills. "MSPAP is not a subject; it's a way of thinking," said Greer.

Upstairs at the sprawling school, for example, art teacher Ledell Flynn is leading fifth-graders in a project to design and market a new line of tennis shoes. This is unlike art lessons of old. Students are assigned to write letters to their parents telling them what they're doing. They have to work as teams— teamwork is a major component of MSPAP—to design the shoes and create commercials to attract buyers. "Persuasive essays are a part of MSPAP," says

Aaron Savage, 10, sounding wise beyond his years. "They've helped me with my writing." Aaron and many of his classmates are voluntarily attending a 3-day-a-week after-school MSPAP Academy.

But if Maryland teachers and principals feel the hot breath of MSPAP and complain about having to spend too much time worrying about the test, things are going to get more stressful as the K–16 initiative proceeds. End-of-course assessments for high school students were being field-tested by 1999. Beginning with the class of 2005, students will have to pass tests in English, government, algebra (or geometry), and—at the discretion of local school systems—biology, in order to receive a diploma. Ultimately, Grasmick said optimistically, "Our exit examinations are going to be the colleges' entrance examinations."

Meanwhile, teachers, professors, and business leaders have worked together to raise the bars even higher in elementary–secondary education. In the summer of 1999 the state board of education approved a set of "content standards" to replace the old curriculum "framework" and specify what students from kindergarten through twelfth grade should know in the major subjects. The Abell Foundation in Baltimore, which financed the writing of the content standards, withheld $100,000 until state curriculum writers put more teeth in the math, history, and geography guidelines. They had been termed "flabby and vague" by the Thomas B. Fordham Foundation, a national group that analyzes academic standards state by state.

Dealing with Teacher Education

Teacher education may be the toughest nut to crack. Maryland's education colleges are a source of frustration for the K–16 planners, who see difficulties on several fronts. The education schools, they say, have been slow to update their programs to meet the high standards of the National Council for the Accreditation of Teacher Education (NCATE), as required by a new state law. They've failed to keep up with the latest education research and to reach out to arts and sciences experts on their own campuses. Maryland tried to promote improvement by seting the nation's second-highest passing rate on Praxis, the successor test to the National Teachers Examination. Only Virginia has a higher passing standard. In other words, higher standards for elementary and secondary students depend on higher standards for those who are going to teach them.

Grasmick made no secret of her disappointment, and she was particularly critical of the two largest education schools, Towson University in the Baltimore metropolitan area and the University of Maryland in College Park. The superintendent lobbied for mandated NCATE accreditation, led the move to double from two to four the number of reading courses required for elementary teacher certification, and insisted on playing a role in the appointment of education deans at the public institutions. "As in most organizations," said Grasmick, "there are issues of power and control, and some of the deans [of education] saw K–16 as an invasion of their turf. This wasn't by any means a case of everyone saying, 'Oh, I embrace the idea, and whatever the collaborative leadership envisions, we're all in support of it!'"

College Park was particularly resistant. Already smarting from a reorganization in 1989 that made the flagship campus the equal of 10 other institutions in the university system, some College Park leaders saw in the K–16 collaborative still more leveling. "College Park is getting over it," said Howard P. Rawlings, the powerful chairman of the Maryland House Appropriations Committee. "They'll be OK once they realize that the world isn't going to collapse."

Langenberg, the university chancellor who first broached the K–16 idea in 1993, said he "learned early on that it's the teachers, dummy. So many of our teachers are graduates of our teacher-training institutions that it's incumbent on us to improve the quality of teacher education. A growing body of research shows that the controlling factor in student performance is the quality of teaching." The chancellor, a physicist by training, cited statistics that demonstrated the extent of the problem: Nationwide, about half of high school math and science teachers are under- or unqualified to teach the subjects. The figure is 70% in rural and urban districts. "This is absolutely scandalous," said Langenberg. "These people don't know enough math and science, and it's not the responsibility of schools of education to teach them. It's the responsibility of math and science departments. This is where we need a whole lot of work."

At Towson, which closed its laboratory school years ago, many education professors spend little time in schools and even less time conferring with colleagues outside their department. There are exceptions. Pat Waters, a 34-year veteran, wears out a set of brakes every year visiting Baltimore County public schools with her students, who she believes will best learn about teaching by observing good teachers in the classroom. On a Sunday in November, she returns late from professional meetings in New Orleans, reading student papers on the plane. Early the next morning she's observing a kindergarten class with two students, juniors who are just beginning the coursework for a major in early childhood education. Back in her campus office after teaching an evening class, she is exhausted and a little disappointed. A mention of Piaget in class has drawn blank stares. "Most of them have taken psychology," she says. "You wonder what they teach over there."

Judith S. Shapiro, the University of Maryland K–16 project director, said there was little inducement for college faculty to talk to teachers, or vice versa.

Although the two are doing similar work, they don't share a "common culture," Shapiro said, "and there are few financial incentives for either side to cross over." Still, Shapiro believed that K–16 was "changing the climate in Maryland."

A Coppin State College faculty meeting in August 1999 showed how the climate was changing. Coppin's faculty met to discuss the new state curriculum standards and the role of academia in forging and enforcing them. There was mutual suspicion in the Coppin cafeteria that day. Coppin is a small school and faculty members are not strangers to each other, but this was a case where arts and sciences, higher up in the traditional hierarchy, were seen as stepping on the teacher educators' turf. In a panel discussion, Gilbert Oganji, a chemist, reached out to save the day. He told his colleagues that he sat on the 24-member state K–16 Leadership Council because he believed in a united approach to education for all Marylanders. "You're the practitioners," he told the teacher educators comfortingly. "We in science are not. We leave that up to you. I'm the guy who counts the feathers on the turkey. Professors like me, especially in science, weren't hired because they were good teachers." The education professors were relieved. "I think it was a good way to start the year," said Francis Kober, a long-time Coppin professor who is deeply involved in the college's effort to operate a nearby public school.

Equalizing Opportunity

Equal opportunity is an equally thorny issue, and it is an issue inextricably tied to efforts to raise standards. Poorly prepared high school graduates flood Maryland colleges, and the 2-year community colleges enroll the majority of students in need of catching up. Remedial rates are staggering; 88% of freshmen at Baltimore City Community College require remedial work in mathematics. Moreover, a disproportionate number of the remedial students are Black. Nearly a half-century after the Supreme Court's historic *Brown* decision, Maryland's African American college graduation rates lag badly behind those of Whites. Of those who do go on to college, 57% choose community colleges, and few of them graduate or transfer to 4-year schools.

In April 1999, the Southern Education Foundation, a respected civil rights monitor, issued *Miles to Go*, a report on the status of minorities in Maryland higher eduction. "Each sector of education is linked to the others," the report said. "What happens to students at one level inevitably affects their performance at the next." Said Robert A. Kronley, senior consultant to the foundation: "Maryland has many of the problems of other states, but at least it has done something many of the other states haven't done: It has admitted it has the problems."

Added Ogonji of Coppin State, a historically Black school and major educator of Maryland teachers: "The toughest issue is equity, and it's a question of standards. If you make the argument that we need to raise standards, then everyone should be on a level playing field. Unfortunately, they're not. All of the schools aren't going to be equal, and I don't see effective solutions on the horizon. It begins to look like something very drastic and immediate will have to be done."

By late 1999, the K–16 partnership could claim some successes, even some unexpected triumphs:

- In 1988, Maryland managed to align the high school graduation requirements and minimum course requirements (but, significantly, not course content) needed for admission to the 11–campus University System of Maryland.
- Agreement was reached on the basic elements of a C essay—a writing example that would get a passing grade from high school and college teachers. The agreement surprised most observers; to reach it, a committee of 13 professors and teachers labored for 2 years and produced a 24-page document, followed by a glossary and 16-page appendix.
- Community colleges and 4-year colleges agreed on a uniform student transfer policy, thus taking a step toward the goal of K–16 seamlessness.
- Professional development schools, the movement of the moment in teacher education, are proliferating. Student teachers from Coppin, Towson University, and Johns Hopkins University, among others, take a page from medical education, pursuing internships in public schools under the watchful eyes of professors.
- And, finally, under the K–16 umbrella, schools and colleges are joining in a number of projects. Johns Hopkins University, long accused of being aloof from the rough-and-tumble of the public schools, established a Center for Reading Excellence in partnership with its rehabilitation hospital, the Kennedy Krieger Institute, and the state education department. Hopkins also combined with historically Black Morgan State University, the University of Maryland, Baltimore County, and Baltimore city schools to help train urban teachers with a $12.6 million federal grant.

One of the smaller but exemplary K–16 projects also involves Hopkins. The Partners in Education Teaching and Learning Program pairs two poor Baltimore inner-city schools with two wealthier schools in suburban Howard County. The four schools have access to the expertise of Hopkins and help from the university's graduate student interns. In another kind of collaboration, business and education leaders are working on a common high school transcript, and the Maryland Business Roundtable for Education, one of the

K–16 partners, has mounted a campaign to encourage employers to inspect transcripts before making hiring decisions.

As president of the Washington-based Education Trust, an organization dedicated to collaboration between public schools and higher education, Kati Haycock has been in a position to watch K–16 play out in Maryland. "They've been remarkably successful, and they're out front of most states," said Haycock, adding that 35 to 40 communities are in one stage or another of building a K–16 strategy and 13 or 14 states are working on statewide plans. Haycock and others were quick to attribute whatever success Maryland had to the triumvirate at the top—Florestano, Grasmick, and Langenberg. But this strength of Maryland's arrangement is also, paradoxically, its weakness. The partnership exists on handshakes among the three appointed officials, who have known each other for years. The partnership could collapse if any of the three were no longer in place. It will be put to the test now, with Florestano's retirement in the summer of 2000.

"Education is very political," Langenberg said. "All it takes is a change of governor, state superintendent, or governing system head, and the circumstances for K–16 can vanish overnight." This explained why Langenberg, through his position as president of the National Association of System Heads, worked to spread the K–16 concept to other states. It's the philosophy of Christian missionaries, he said: "If you spread the gospel to many places, it will live on if you fail in some of them." Secretary Florestano thought that the K–16 partnership would have to be legislatively sanctioned, particularly if it is to have greater success in raising money for incentive grants. That's good advice for other states, particularly if education leaders are subject to the winds of politics.

These are some of the other policy implications drawn from the Maryland experience:

• Give all the partners an equal voice in decision making and, as much as possible, an equal share of the resources. Maryland goes so far as to rotate chairmanship of the K–16 advisory council among Florestano, Grasmick, and Langenberg.

• Seek a steady source of income. The partnership doesn't need a bureaucracy, but it needs a line in the state budget to give it a chance for long-range planning and stability.

• A partnership works best if momentum flows from the bottom up and the top down at the same time. State officials and university presidents have to provide leadership (as was recommended in a recent report from the American Council on Education), but faculty must deliver the curriculum, the courses, and the instruction that will enable students to perform.

• The three toughest issues are equal opportunity, alignment of high school and college curriculum, and teacher education. Teacher preparation and educational research must be strengthened in academe. Start early on these issues; they'll take longer to address.

• Try not to forget the students, which is what the effort is all about.

• Expect setbacks. It's a long, hard, and sometimes unpleasant journey that will never reach the promised land. But there are great rewards along the way.

CHAPTER 7

PASS: Oregon's New Path to College

William Graves

Students sit stunned one morning in Mimi Alkire's pre-calculus class as she describes how the rules for getting into college are about to change. Oregon's new admissions process, she tells her students at Cleveland High School in Portland, will judge them on performance rather than on grades and course credits. "The requirement is to meet proficiency in English," Alkire says. "If you can do that in less than 4 years, you qualify for college." Justin, slouched in a desk near the window, knits his brow and slowly rotates a sucker in the air as though mimicking the thoughts churning through his head. "So if you get a 4.0 grade-point average, but don't do well on the proficiencies, you don't go to college?" he asks. "Yes," says Alkire bluntly. "Eventually, there won't be grade-point averages."

Alkire is describing the Oregon University System's emerging Proficiency-Based Admission Standards System, or PASS, which could revolutionize the way colleges in the state choose their students, eventually becoming the cloth that binds public schools to higher education in a single, seamless system geared to academic standards. The new system also may shape the rigor, content, and substance of instruction in high school classrooms. It already has affected classrooms in 56 Oregon high schools, where trained teachers such as Alkire are beginning to help students meet admission proficiencies. "Almost everything we do this year is PASS-related," Alkire says.

She gives her students practice with a problem typical of what will be used to judge their proficiency. It requires students to come up with a functional equation that tells them how much a lobster dinner costs at a restaurant where three lobster and two steak dinners cost a total $78, but three steak and two lobster dinners cost $72. One girl, wearing Hawaiian flowers in her hair for Spirit Week, pokes at her calculator. In an instant, she produces an answer. But it's not good enough, Alkire tells her. Proficiency demands more. She must show, step-by-step, using a formula and mathematical symbols, a strategy for solving the problem. She must also use an alternative strategy, say graphing the function, to verify her answer. "There is nothing wrong with guess and check," says Alkire. "But it is not a very high-level way of solving the problem."

If all goes according to plan, Oregon's 7 universities and its 17 community colleges will use problems such as this rather than course credits and grade-point averages (GPAs) to judge students for admission. Beginning in the fall of 2001, the system will start a phase-in of performance standards that will become mandatory in 2005. No one knows whether the public higher education system can pull off such a fundamental shift. David Conley, a lanky University of Oregon education professor, heads the effort. He gives it 50–50 odds. "It is totally feasible; it is totally doable," said the intense, energetic educator. "But it is a profound change in a system that is not enamored with profound change."

As the century turned, PASS remained more idea than practice. Many educators and most parents and students remained totally in the dark about proficiency standards. The new admissions system depends heavily on teachers, who must learn how to judge student work samples, exhibition, and tests using the same criteria. This departure from traditional grading requires extensive training, new student transcripts, and complex system changes. Teachers fear it means yet another workload. Administrators, preoccupied with other public school reforms, remain skeptical. The Oregon Board of Higher Education rarely discusses it. State leaders have issued no policy guidelines to promote it. Conley has found his effort to connect the higher education and public school systems fraught with complications, like trying to weave together a Turkish tapestry with one from China.

Nevertheless, no state has moved deeper into proficiency-based admissions than Oregon, according to the American Association of State Colleges and Universities. Conley has trudged for more than 6 years in the virgin wilderness of true collaboration between higher education and the public schools. He was pressing forward with a $1-million annual budget and an 11-person staff; he had a pilot project to work on proficiencies with 140 teachers and the 7,000 students in their classrooms. This was the infrastructure he was using by the end of the 1990s to test and refine a new system. And he had commitment from the top. "I admit to being a skeptic when this first surfaced," said Joseph W. Cox, chancellor of the Oregon University System. "But I have to tell you, the idea grows on you. I have gone from being a skeptic initially to being a passionate advocate."

Under the standards, students will be judged on what they know and can do rather than on grades and coursework. Instead of simply chalking up 2 years of Spanish credits, for example, a student will be required to speak and write Spanish at a defined level of proficiency. How he reaches that level is less important. He might learn it by taking 4 years of high school Spanish, or he might learn it as a foreign-exchange student in Costa Rica. What will matter to Oregon universities is that he is proficient. And these are not minimum standards. Consider the following proficiencies from mathematics, English, and science, which require students to be able to do the following:

- Represent and solve problems with two- and three-dimensional geometric models, properties of figures, analytic geometry, and trigonometry
- Analyze literary forms, elements, devices, and themes to interpret and critique literary texts
- Design and conduct experiments using principles of scientific inquiry, investigative process, scientific instruments, and technology. Collect and analyze data, critique experimental designs, and communicate scientific problems, results, and arguments

Working with the High Schools

The PASS developers are aligning their proficiency standards with the high school standards that the Oregon Department of Education is creating. The hope is that eventually Oregon high schools will have exit or graduation standards that resemble or mirror the higher education proficiency standards. Then, by meeting the standards to graduate, a student will simultaneously meet those for admission to the state universities.

Oregon's college admissions officers, frustrated by the murky portraits that emerged from grade transcripts and SAT scores, began searching for more precise ways to judge students in the late 1980s. The catalyst for action came in 1991, when the legislature passed a sweeping public school reform act that called for setting performance standards at grades 3, 5, 8, and 10. It also called for creating two new high school credentials based on standards called certificates of mastery. Students would be expected to earn their Certificate of Initial Mastery (CIM) at about the end of their sophomore year. During their final two years of high school, they would go on to earn a Certificate of Advanced Mastery (CAM), which would be based on higher academic standards and some job experience connected with career goals.

In July of 1993, under orders from Governor Barbara Roberts, the state boards of education and higher education met in Ashland to improve communication and cooperation between the two systems. During the meeting, educators told the boards that if the higher education sector could specify what students were expected to know and be able to do when they entered college, the public schools would make sure that's what students learned. The two boards immediately embraced the offer. Conley, a consultant to the higher education board, was asked to draft a list of the skills and knowledge that colleges expected to see in their freshmen. Thus, in a 10-minute spell of enthusiasm, almost on a whim, PASS was born, and Conley was put in charge.

Conley and his staff set out to write PASS proficiencies so that students could simultaneously meet them when they fulfilled standards for their CIM and CAM. He employed teachers to design, test, and refine all 33 PASS proficiencies. By the fall of 1999, teachers in the 56 pilot schools were collecting work from 4,000 teenagers, including some freshmen, to evaluate their performance in math, English, and science. They had done the same for 3,000 students the previous year.

Students who meet standards will get certificates that they can append like merit badges to their college applications. In the fall of 2001, students will be able to replace course credits with proficiencies to meet admissions requirements for English and math. They will be able to do the same in science in 2002, in social science in 2003, and in the arts in 2004. Students will have the option during these years of ignoring the standards and relying on grades, course credits, and SAT scores to win their way into the system. But freshmen seeking entry to the Oregon University System in the fall of 2005 will be expected to meet proficiency standards in all subjects, including a second language.

The Impact of PASS

Advocates say PASS will give higher education a more precise way of judging applicants and will give parents a clearer picture of what children need to learn to go to college. Grades are unreliable, skewed by inflation, and they vary from school to school, even class to class, so a student might earn a C from one teacher and an A from another for the same work. Students are led to believe that they are doing fine, and then national tests reveal that they perform below standard, says Conley. "We've absolutely deceived and cheated them," he says.

PASS attempts to end deception by requiring all teachers to grade students using the same sophisticated, five-part scale that classifies the quality of work as follows: N, not meeting proficiency; W, working toward proficiency; M, meets proficiency; and H, high-level mastery of proficiency. The top category, E, exemplary, is reserved for the 2% to 5% of students who soar into the academic stratosphere. The goal is to ensure that an essay deemed proficient by a teacher in Ashland also will be judged proficient by a teacher in Astoria. Then Oregon college admissions officers in 6 years would get transcripts that show consistent student proficiency levels rather than vague grades. Admissions officers were initially skeptical about PASS but now expect that it will "be a better gauge of what students know when they come to us," says Martha Pitts, director of admissions for the University of Oregon.

PASS may also affect standards, content, and instruction in high school classrooms. PASS designers, teachers mostly, looked at CIM standards as they created proficiencies. Now the State Department of Education has PASS proficiencies on the easel as it designs standards for the Certificate of Advanced Mastery—essentially high school exit standards. What's more, teachers are ratcheting up the rigor of their classes to make sure students meet PASS standards. During a summer workshop at the University of Oregon, one teacher told Conley she didn't think her students would learn enough in her Functions, Statistics, and Trigonometry class to meet all criteria for the PASS probability and statistics proficiency. "I'm going to ask you to modify what you do enough so kids get the proficiencies," Conley said. "The first year you do this, you're going to struggle."

Teachers piloting PASS say once they adjust to the new system, their teaching improves. Kate Kennedy of Ashland High School says PASS has made her job tougher, but her science students write more and think more deeply. "Teachers do not want life to be easier," Kennedy said. "They want their lives to be more effective." During a workshop for PASS teachers at the University of Oregon in August 1999, Conley, dressed in jeans and a button-down shirt, strolls around a circular table, where questions written by teachers on small cards have been laid neatly in concentric circles like some kind of fortune wheel. He's heard most of the questions before: Will CAM have any tie in with PASS (You keep pushing CIM and Pass)? How to cover all the proficiencies without burning out students and causing them to turn off? How do I cover all the content and do the inquiry activities, too?

At a table nearby, Catherine Gray of West Linn High in a Portland suburb and four other math teachers try to determine what students must do to prove they could meet a single PASS proficiency on functions. They can see that students need to produce a portfolio of evidence involving multiple work samples from more than one activity and probably from more than one class. Students may be able to learn how to define functions in Algebra I, but they won't be able to really analyze functions until they reach Algebra II. Gray sees a "paper nightmare" in trying to collect enough samples over several years to prove a student has demonstrated proficiency. Oregon schools got a taste of such complexity in issuing Certificates of Initial Mastery to sophomores who met English and mathematics standards in the spring of 1999.

Schools were to use a combination of test scores and work samples to determine whether students met standards. But by the end of the school year, students still did not know whether they had earned their certificates because schools were buried in paperwork.

Conley knows one of his most daunting and critical challenges will be selling PASS to public school educators, parents, and students. Unless he can show teachers that they can judge students for PASS with the same work samples and tests they use for CIM or CAM, the new system "will die under its own weight," says James Sager, president of the Oregon Education Association. It could also die if teachers don't work to understand the use of consistent proficiency criteria rather than grades to judge student work. "Humans have to engage in this," said Conley. "You can't just do what you are told here. You have to truly understand what adequate performance looks like."

Collaboration between higher education and public schools has been "incredibly painful," Conley lamented. The state Department of Education was a reluctant partner, he said, and neither the governor's office nor the legislature offered policy guidance to foster a stronger joint venture. Different bureaucracies had different goals, and the people within them were not used to working with one another. "Sharing resources is almost impossible," Conley said. "Progress is glacial. It is absolutely draining. It requires commitment at a fundamental level."

Nevertheless, the PASS project showed enough progress to catch the eyes of university systems in other states, some of which are also plunging into proficiency-based admissions. A 50-state survey by the State Higher Education Executive Officers identified 11 states that were studying a proficiency-based admission link between public high school and college. Maryland, Colorado, Washington, and Wisconsin have all made commitments to developing proficiency-based admission approaches. Maryland high school teachers, for example, worked with higher education faculty in developing the state's Core Learning Goals, which students must meet to graduate beginning in 2004. The goals are aligned with the University System of Maryland admissions requirements.

The Future of College Admissions

These various projects raise questions about whether college admissions will end up varying from state to state, producing a Tower of Babel, said Travis Reindl, policy analyst for the American Association of State Colleges and Universities. Another question emerged in Oregon over whether PASS standards would end up being too high. "When the university system fully implements PASS, [admissions officers] will find they cannot admit very many in-state freshmen," said Sue Hagmeier, member of the Portland School Board.

Chancellor Cox called that conclusion "defeatist and condescending." He said that the teachers who wrote the PASS standards would not deliberately create a system in which no one could succeed. What's more, he added, young people clearly understand the need for high skills and knowledge to compete in the modern workplace and will aspire to clear standards. He predicted that PASS would "have the effect of raising the horizon and expectation levels of kids who right now do not even have [college] on the screen." Mark Endsley, who coached other PASS teachers, said that one lesson he learned through teaching to science proficiencies in Gresham, a Portland suburb, was that students could handle more than schools usually require of them. He said: "Teachers say, 'I can't believe the level of performance of our students.'" Even if PASS were to reduce the number of qualified freshman, more of them probably would survive their 4 years of college because they all would be solidly prepared, higher education leaders say. Currently, nearly half drop out.

Five juniors at Cleveland High in Portland who earned some proficiencies in math and English are generally supportive of PASS but wary of its demands and skeptical of its benefits. They said that the various tests and work samples are tedious, stressful, and time-consuming. Eric Anderson, 16, said he rewrote a paper five times for English before it met the standard. But he admitted that it forced him to work harder. Julia Carr, 16, said that she hated having to verify her math problems. "I have to find a completely new way to do what I just did," she said.

But the students all talk about CIM and PASS as one and the same, as in many cases they are—a sign that the two systems are becoming integrated. Cox speculated that a truly seamless system would also become a more fluid one, allowing some students to enter college after only 2 or 3 years of high school and some also to complete college faster. And the higher, more reliable standards would allow universities to scrap remedial courses, redesign the freshman year, and spend a higher proportion of their money on the junior and senior years, which now are shortchanged because of heavy underclassmen costs.

The university system, then, could use PASS to dramatically reshape secondary and higher education, said Cox, by serving as a hydraulic slowly lifting the academic achievement levels of all high school students. Wherever PASS ultimately takes Oregon's schools and colleges, teaching to proficiencies has already been worthwhile in helping teachers draw quality work from their students, said Diane Smith, an English teacher from Albany. "I just know that when I do this," she said, "it is better for kids."

CHAPTER 8

GEORGIA'S P–16 INITIATIVE

Ernie Suggs

Metropolitan Avenue in Atlanta is anything but metropolitan. With its bars, strip joints, hookers, and incessant crime, the avenue has developed a reputation as a place that many people want to avoid. But it is also the home of Atlanta Metropolitan College, a 2-year institution within the University System of Georgia that provides affordable and accessible higher educational opportunities for a primarily African American student body from Atlanta. Only 5 minutes from downtown, Atlanta Metro, as it is known, is a college that often teems with adolescents who look too young to be on campus.

These students attend a Saturday Academy for ninth- and tenth-graders. They receive classroom instruction and tutorial support every other Saturday in their regular high school subjects. Their parents participate in sessions of their own to familiarize them with educational resources in the community that are available to help students. This instruction is possible because Atlanta Metro is a partner in the Metro-Atlanta local P–16 council and serves as a Post-Secondary Enrichment Program (PREP) site for the Atlanta area. So, while television screens elsewhere in the city are filled with cartoons and southeastern football games, while other teenagers are playing basketball or football or wandering the malls, 200 students, most of them Black, spend their time trying to improve their academic preparation. "This program is making a tremendous difference," said Gary McGaha, site coordinator for Metro-Atlanta PREP. "We have success stories of students whose grades have improved because of this program. The idea here is to get these students prepared for college."

All across Georgia, PREP sites offer supplemental activities in academic, social, and cultural enrichment during regular school hours, after school, and on Saturdays to middle and high school students who need this extra boost. Using matching state and private funds, these services are provided through collaborations of 25 University System institutions, 20 technical institutes, more than 250 businesses and community organizations, and 409 middle and high schools in nine geographical areas throughout the state.

Albany State University, for instance, one of four institutions in Site IX that serves students in southwest Georgia, conducted a 2-week intensive residential summer program with a rigorous academic curriculum. The severity of the at-risk factors plaguing the majority of these children indicated that they would be best served by living on the campus for the duration of the 2-week program. Activities began at 6:00 in the morning and concluded at 9:00 at night. Included in the daily regimen were classes in core academic subjects, physical fitness, modules on hygiene and safety, drug and alcohol prevention classes, and elective cultural enrichment activities.

In another example of PREP's efforts, the summer program at Floyd College in Rome emphasized learning to help others. Students participated in a Volunteer Training course to prod them to realize that almost everyone is capable of making a contribution to his or her community. The students did service in a day-care center, a soup kitchen, a health clinic, and a nursing home; they learned about different human service careers. A parent wrote, "to sum it all up, this program exemplifies what life is all about, to gain education to achieve and then to give service to your fellow man."

PREP, which was designed to get young people ready for higher education, was a pet project of Stephen Portch, chancellor of the University System of Georgia. The program strives to prepare students to meet the higher admissions requirements for college that will be in effect in 2001. "With the overall strategy of raising admission standards, the least likely to hear about it are those who are at-risk," Portch said. "It is important to make a commitment to that segment of our society." Since 1996, more than 30,000 students across Georgia have participated in PREP. President Bill Clinton cited it as a model program. In 1998, the results of a formative program evaluation indicated that students, middle school teachers, and administrators expressed high satisfaction with the services. PREP still must meet the challenge of increasing parents' involvement in the education of their children, which many experts think is a key element in the success of students.

Supporters of PREP have been encouraged by the willingness of many of the program's tutors/mentors to involve themselves in the program beyond their assigned duties. The favorable response of some businesses in providing such resources for the programs, such as meals, equipment, and facilities, has also encouraged proponents. It remains to be seen, though, how this will all add up in 2001 and during later years in ensuring that the students of the sort who have fared most poorly in the past are ready for post-secondary education.

The Need for Intervention

PREP is just one of the three strands of work within a statewide initiative in Georgia called the Pre-School through Post-Secondary (P–16) Initiative. The three strands of this effort to raise standards through closer school-college collaboration are the following:

- Alignment of expectations (standards), curriculum, and assessment for students, from preschool through postsecondary education
- Teacher quality—having a qualified teacher in every Georgia public school classroom
- Supplemental programs for seventh-through twelfth-grade students in at-risk situations who would benefit from extra support in order to be prepared for postsecondary education

Many college-age students in Georgia found themselves ill prepared for higher education in the 1990s. The state's SAT average of 969 was 47 points below the national average. Furthermore, in excess of 20% of the state's high school graduates entering postsecondary education required remedial education. There were gaps between what students knew leaving high school and what they needed to know for college, technical institute, or employment. There was also a gap between what teachers expected of students and what the teachers themselves knew of the subjects that they were assigned to teach. P–16 strives to close these various gaps.

Based on the theory that the gaps were exacerbated by a fragmented educational system that was missing links between schools and colleges, Georgia in 1995 embarked on one of the most ambitious efforts in the country to tie elementary and secondary schools more closely to postsecondary education. It was called the P–16 Initiative. An array of educational agencies across the state came together and, along with businesses desperate for a better-equipped work force, signed on in hopes of reaping long-term benefits from a better-educated employees. "For all students to attain high, clearly articulated academic standards, they must attend superior schools where all teachers are qualified and committed to student learning," said Jan Kettlewell, assistant vice-chancellor for academic affairs for the University System of Georgia's Board of Regents and co-facilitator for the Georgia P–16 Initiative.

In 1995, Governor Zell Miller created the State P–16 Council by executive order, charging the members with improving the academic achievement of students at all levels. "Our whole educational process must become both stronger and more seamless," Miller said at the swearing-in ceremony for the new Council. "And the only way that can happen is if our schools, colleges, and technical institutes work together." The State Council is co-chaired through a rotation system of the four heads of the Office of School Readiness, the State Department of Education, the Department of Technical and Adult Education, and the University System. Membership includes individuals from postsecondary education, P–12 education, the legislature, youth advocate groups, various businesses, and the community.

The Council meets quarterly and provides overall coordination and leadership for the P–16 Initiative at both the state and local levels. Subcommittees appointed to carry out the work forward recommendations to the Council for action. Despite the rotating chairs, there was concern among some partners that the University System was driving the Initiative. Kettlewell rejected this notion. "There are some individuals who see it driven by the university," she said. "But the most important thing is focusing on issues that cut across the state that one education agency cannot solve alone."

But the Georgia P–16 Council has no real power and can only make recommendations. This lack of power raises the question of how such a body can bring about change. Critics, mostly within the K–12 system, point out that P–16 has no authority under the state's constitution. However, Miller's successor as governor, Roy Barnes, laid the groundwork in 1999 for a shake-up in the power dynamics as a step toward achieving P–16's goals. The 64-member Education Reform Study Commission, which Barnes created and chaired, explored some of the same issues already brought to the surface by the State P–16 Council—curriculum alignment and standards—but did so in a much more visible way. Furthermore, the Education Reform Study Commission recommended the creation of a coordinating council that would bring together, with the governor as chair, the top officials of the main agencies controlling Georgia's fragmented education from the preschool through the postsecondary level. By having the governor play an active role in the coordinating council, which could replace the P–16 Council, all players, presumably, would have to become active and willing participants.

Taking the Effort Down to the Grassroots

Early on it was recognized that work at just the state level, while necessary, was insufficient. Attention had to be given to the grassroots. Thus, 15 local/regional P–16 councils were established in 1997 to build support and to pilot new directions for the effort. This became the P–16 Network. The local councils worked to spur change in their geographic regions. The Network is the vehicle used for maintaining close communications and building cross-regional relationships among participants. "P–16 in Georgia is the most comprehensive initiative of its kind," Kettlewell said. "Maryland has a similar program, but we are the only state with state and local P–16 boards. Once we got into it, it was clear that the partnerships needed to be broader." The membership within the 15 local councils included 29 University System colleges and universities (out of 34), 147 school districts (out of 180), 23 technical institutes (out of 34), 23 private schools, 80 businesses, 41 public agencies, and representatives from the community. Local councils competed for challenge grants to implement their plans in either or both of the first two strands of P–16 work. Using state and private funds, 19 multiyear challenge grants were awarded to local councils.

The University System provided the seed money to get the local P–16 councils off the ground and charged them with the development of unique plans to achieve the P–16 mission by focusing on teacher quality and/or alignment of expectations (standards), curriculum, and assessment for students. But provision of this assistance helped further the concern that the P–16 Initiative was being controlled by the University System as a "superboard" imposing itself on local school boards. Portch said that perception was something the Initiative wrestled with from the beginning. The P–16 Council came out with this statement to address such concerns about its role:

> P–16 Councils are broad-based, voluntary, representative groups of pre-school through 12th grade and post-secondary educators, school board members, youth advocate organizations, community members, legislative and business leaders who are collaborating at the state and local/regional levels to promote and recommend changes in public educational systems that will improve student success at all levels. Recommendations are forwarded to the proper authorities and governing boards. P–16 Councils are not governance structures. P–16 Councils have no authority in policy or law.

Dealing with Teacher Quality

Soon after the Council was created, the P–16 Initiative lifted teacher quality to a priority. In 1996, Georgia became a partner state with the National Commission on Teaching and America's Future. The teacher education subcommittee of the P–16 Council was charged with preparing a report to take stock of the status of teaching in Georgia. The report was completed in 1998. It found serious imbalances in the supply of teachers for some subjects and for some geographic areas, a problem compounded by the tendency of colleges of education to turn out too many graduates in some fields, such as early childhood education, and too few in others, such as the sciences.

The Professional Standards Commission, a partner in the Initiative, implemented a regulation to allow for the expansion of experimental alternative teacher preparation programs. This effort consciously sought collaboration among higher education institutions, local schools, and regional associations. In 1998, the Commission approved the first alternative teacher preparation program. At the same time, the Board of Regents adopted the Principles and Actions for the Preparation of Educators for the Schools for all public teacher preparation institutions. The Principles included a guarantee that a struggling teacher could be sent back to college at the System's expense for retraining. The need for such further education was underscored by the fact that about 10% of high school teachers and up to 45% of middle school teachers taught outside the field for which they were prepared.

In June of 1999, the P–16 Council released a follow-up report to serve as an implementation plan for the recommendations made in the original plan. This later report, entitled *Georgia's Plan for Having a Qualified Teacher in Every Public School Classroom*, included the following proposals:

- Offering incentives aimed at off-setting the high attrition rate for teachers in their first 3 years of teaching
- Implementing pilot programs to test the effectiveness of giving stipends to attract teachers for fields with teacher shortages or for regions with shortages
- Raising the admission requirements for teacher preparation programs
- Factoring student achievement into the decision of whether a person's professional teaching certificate is renewed
- Requiring teachers to take at least 15 semester hours of college study in any subject they teach

Work at the local level on teacher quality is an important part of the Network. Seven local councils tried to align teacher preparation course content with the content teachers are expected to cover and the instructional strategies they are expected to use in P–12 classrooms. Five councils strengthened teaching field experiences by increasing time spent in the schools and providing teacher candidates with experiences that exposed them to student diversity. Six councils provided comprehensive and responsive professional development for their area teachers.

An intriguing innovation of the Council was its Performance Assessment for College and Technical School (PACTS). This feature came in conjunction with the alignment of standards and curriculum. PACTS aimed to ensure that all students who graduate from high school are prepared for postsecondary education or employment. If the program, still in the pilot stages, is successful and approved, there is a plan to scale up the use of the assessment system for statewide admission. PACTS would make clearer what level of academic work is needed to be successful. Four local P–16 councils are working together to pilot this program in their regions. Local high schools volunteered to be a part of this trial. "While the movement to academic standards is only a recent undertaking by school systems and states, there already is evidence that setting standards leads to improved student achievement," said Pamela Hertzog of the South Georgia regional P–16 council.

For the most part, P–16 has made some real progress, although there have been bumps in the road. One of these has been the fact that while P–16 has worked to change attitudes, it had to walk through a minefield consisting of the skeptical professors and proponents of local control in the public schools or state department of education. "Our work involves the commitment of many participants," said Kettlewell, adding that implementing a strategy such as P–16 requires leadership, an investment of seed money, and a clear recognition of the problems. "There is always a tendency for people to want to implement projects. When local and state gets together, we are so ingrained to implement a project as being the answer. That is not always right. We have to change the system so that we can help everybody."

An infrastructure must be built to support the needed changes. Through the Network it is possible to form a statewide consensus on "essential elements" of P–16 work and to monitor progress statewide. Georgia allowed local councils to work on teacher quality and/or alignment. All councils probably should have worked on alignment issues before moving to teacher quality. By first aligning the "student system" and closing the expectations gap, the "student system" could then be used as the target for setting standards for teachers. This approach would offer greater assurance that teachers would have the depth as well as breadth in specific subject fields to instruct students in such a way that students can achieve the higher expectations at each level. While important for the cohorts of PREP students served throughout Georgia, these experiences must lead to systemic changes in schools.

Today's society requires more educated individuals than in the past. Students who graduate from high schools in Georgia and elsewhere must be prepared for a smooth transition into college or the work force. All levels of education must be aligned with one another, and performance at each level has to be higher than previously required. At the same time, Georgia has to put educational programs in place to ensure equity for students from diverse backgrounds as they work to meet the higher standards. The state hopes that the collaborative structure of the Georgia P–16 Initiative can further this effort.

PART IV

Teachers

Among the most fertile areas for collaboration between schools and colleges is anything involving teachers. Those who teach in elementary and secondary schools all were students in institutions of higher education before taking over classrooms. Furthermore, in many cases schoolteachers, once they are on the job, turn to colleges and universities for the professional development that will enable them to hone the craft of teaching. Thus, this study takes a look at one project in which a university and a school system worked together to try to better prepare novices for their classroom duties and another project in which a university and a number of school systems cooperated on behalf of the continuing education of teachers already on the job.

In the first of these case studies, Lonnie Harp examined professional development schools in Cincinnati. These schools, with some of the attributes of teaching hospitals, seek to function as places where young people heading into teaching careers can get a firm grounding under the tutelage of practitioners. Cincinnati embarked on this experiment with the cooperation of the University of Cincinnati (UC), the Cincinnati public schools, and the Cincinnati Federation of Teachers. "It's a huge advantage," one college student said of her experience. "A lot of my friends are jealous of what I got during my time at UC, even though it was an extra year and more money." Yet the success of such ventures depends not just on the institution of higher education but also on the solvency and leadership of the school system itself, not to mention the ongoing goodwill of the teachers' union.

In Mississippi, Jackson State University made a special commitment to boost teaching by reaching out to those already in the field. This three-pronged effort involved a mentoring program to prepare practitioners to seek certification from the National Board of Professional Teaching Standards, a consortium for delivering training in technology and instructional technques to teachers already in classrooms, and an attempt to upgrade teachers of preschool pupils. Monique Fields noted that Jackson State's role was adversely affected by the difficulty of getting the university's faculty members to contribute their expertise to the programs, not an usual experience for an institution of higher education when it comes to working with the schools.

CHAPTER 9

PROFESSIONAL PRACTICE SCHOOLS IN CINCINNATI

Lonnie Harp

As long as educational theories have been presented, dissected, and analyzed at the University of Cincinnati's (UC) education college, Hughes Center High School stood barely a block away, etched into the horizon in grand Gothic splendor. There, behind walls guarded by leering and smirking gargoyles, the education concepts dispensed in mint condition in the nearby college classrooms were fire-tested by the daily discord of a bustling public high school, where they often wound up in shreds. This was where theory collided with practice. Veteran Cincinnati teachers talk about what they learned in college and what they learned in the classroom as if these were altogether different ideas. They use words like "shock" to describe the transition from college to the reality of school. The college and the high school share a ZIP code, but the professors who knew *why* and the teachers at the high school who had to know *how* seemed to speak different languages.

Diane Holderbach is glad the strangers finally met—not only met, but spent years trying to connect the training ground to the proving ground. Holderbach is a novelty: a first-year Algebra I and pre-calculus teacher with a math degree who not only feels at home and effective in her classroom but also speaks up in faculty meetings to discuss curriculum and teaching issues. She is an oddity not only in the eyes of seasoned teachers. At 24, she is even counseling peers, fellow rookie teachers from other colleges who phone her seeking reassurance or help on how to set up a classroom, how to deal with uncooperative students, or how to fit in with an established faculty. "It's a huge advantage. A lot of my friends are jealous of what I got during my time at UC, even though it was an extra year and more money," she said during her daily planning break. "With me being more comfortable, it allows more time to focus on the students' needs. Because I spend so little time having to send people out of the room or to detention, we can do more problems and answer more questions."

The University of Cincinnati became a national leader by connecting its teacher training programs to the public schools, linking theory and practice. In cooperation with the Cincinnati Federation of Teachers and in partnership with the school district, UC students who are preparing for careers in the classroom spend a fifth year of college in one of nine schools—down from eleven schools at the program's peak—across the city that are part of the collaborative training program. The unusual alliance is an example of a growing national movement to upgrade the status of teachers and improve student performance by adding more subject-area know-how and more practical exposure to the traditional training in education theory and teaching methods.

University alumni who have spent their careers as teachers and principals in the Cincinnati schools and witnessed the changes say that recent graduates are vastly more prepared to start teaching than they were before the advent of the model known as professional development schools. A marketplace hungry for new teachers pays its own compliments to the college–union–district initiative. The program is still adjusting to the aggressiveness of suburban schools, which often beat the Cincinnati district to the punch in making job offers to the UC grads whom the city schools worked to cultivate. "These students seem more interested in education, more inclined toward teaching, more aware, and more mature," said Greg Hook, principal of Vine Elementary School, an inner-city school that volunteered to work with the UC interns in part because it attributed its high teacher turnover rate to inadequate preparation. "There's really no comparison with what people got before."

In the schools where it works best, the Cincinnati program embodies what national reformers had expected from professional development schools: that veteran teachers would become more reflective about what and how they teach as they coach college students, that new members of the profession would arrive with a firm grasp of both the theoretical side of education and the reality of school, and that the resulting professional chemistry would invigorate schools to try out new ideas and contemplate how well they reach students.

The Need for Reforms

In Cincinnati, agreement on revamping the university's teacher-training program was preceded by an earlier, almost coincidental, consensus on the need for reforms in teaching by college officials, the teachers' union, and the school district. These ideas took root in Cincinnati as similar conversations about school reform were taking place across the country. In the 1980s, as a series of influential reports on education found the performance of American pupils woeful and raised concerns that too many students were being tracked into general-education courses where mediocrity was the highest standard, some reformers found a culprit besides lax expectations or inadequate financing: Dreary teaching and poorly prepared teachers were also found to be widespread handicaps.

In 1986, the Holmes Group, then a new organization of 50 education deans and top university academic officers throughout the United States, called for abolishing the undergraduate education major in favor of deeper study in subjects teachers planned to teach. The group also recommended a new brand of college classroom that would exemplify strong teaching styles and new connections between colleges and schools. New training programs would be centered at professional development schools comparable to teaching hospitals. A report by the Holmes Group acknowledged such obstacles as the higher costs that would be associated with new approaches. Similar teaching reform ideas were also percolating from the American Federation of Teachers (AFT), which called its collaborations "professional practice schools" (PPS).

These ideas combined in Cincinnati, where a strong AFT-affiliated union was eager to try fresh ideas such as new pay systems, tougher teacher evaluations, and new preparation programs to upgrade teaching. Meanwhile, UC officials were concerned about the quality of their teacher preparation program and were looking at a wholesale redesign. "What made it work especially well in Cincinnati was that this wasn't an idea that just came from the university," said Robert Yinger, the former school–university partnership director at UC who is now dean of the education college at Baylor University in Waco, Texas. "When we sat down with the district to explore the idea, we found the union and the district had already been talking about it and put clauses in their 1988 contract that would allow for it."

The sides built a strong working partnership with incentives for all three participating entities—the university, the school system, and the teachers' union. Yinger and Tom Mooney, president of the Cincinnati Federation of Teachers (CFT), became driving forces behind the plan, which won support from the university's president and top administrators. School superintendent J. Michael Brandt's smooth relations with Mooney helped make the program a cooperative endeavor.

One of the early breakthroughs was an agreement to create paid internship slots for UC teacher education students by "capturing" vacancies when teachers retired. The district could save money while paying interns less than the veterans had received. At the same time, top teachers were cast as mentors for the interns. Cincinnati envisioned two half-time interns splitting each available teaching position and working under the guidance of master teachers, who were being identified as mentors under the CFT's new career-ladder pay system. Some of the program's master teachers became involved in work at the university, even teaching introductory education courses. The college and the school district presented the idea to individual schools, where the staff could vote to join the model. By the fall of 1994, fifth-year interns were ready for their assignments, and four Cincinnati schools launched the new wave in teacher training.

The program is markedly different from traditional teacher education programs in which students start working on education as freshmen and finish their senior year with a 10–week student teaching job, often at an elementary or secondary school of their choice. UC students now apply to the teaching program in the winter term of their third year of college after fulfilling general-education requirements. In their fourth year, the students finish their first major in a discipline other than education while taking their first teaching methods courses. They begin to study classroom management and visit Cincinnati schools. In their fifth year, the students are assigned to their year-long classroom internship while finishing education coursework that includes advanced teaching methods and ethics courses. In addition to stronger subject-area training and more practical experience, the program gives students an education in how urban schools work.

Diane Holderbach, one of the exemplary products of the programs, attended suburban private schools before earning her degree at the University of Cincinnati. She explained that the program helped her build experience and gain confidence in her ability to cope with the unfamiliarity of urban classrooms. In her praise of the program, she echoes many other UC graduates. The professional development schools have largely lived up to their aim of producing teachers with a loyalty to teaching inner-city schoolchildren. Holderbach said she took the job at Hughes Center High because she specifically wanted to continue working in an urban classroom, as she had as a UC student; she also wanted to stay in a school where cultivating good teaching was a priority. The program was replete with positive reviews from graduates and some of the 90 interns who worked in Cincinnati professional practice schools during the 1999–2000 school year. College officials said that the percentage of graduates taking teaching jobs increased and first-year attrition rates dropped for graduates of UC's teachers college, a seeming testament to more serious on-the-job training.

In the Crucible of the Classroom

On the first truly chilly morning of autumn, several children straggled into the doors of Hays Elementary School, late. The crisp weather managed to put everyone in a forgiving mood, and tardy passes were dispensed genially.

Since the heat was not yet turned on in the building, the principal made stops in classrooms to remind children about the importance of layering their clothes to stay warm. One stop was an upstairs combined first- and second-grade class where students were spread everywhere—scattered at tables and sitting or lying on the floor working on a timeline depicting the life of civil rights activist Rosa Parks. There, University of Cincinnati intern Heather McGuire, 22, a lifelong resident of the Cincinnati suburbs, practiced making an orderly transition from one lesson to the next, in this case the weekly spelling test.

After quiet instructions, the class went through its paces, putting away its work and its pencil boxes. "Those of us sitting quietly in our seats will get a piece of paper," McGuire said in the reassuring tones of an airline pilot. The children moving toward their seats were mostly poor and often from homes led by single mothers involved in welfare-to-work programs and strongly interested in their children's success at school, the principal said later. Though McGuire still had 7 months of classroom practice remaining, she was pleased with the expertise she had already gained and her sense that she had shared ownership of this classroom from the start of school. She said that Terry Armstrong, the PPS coordinator at Hays and McGuire's mentor, was the best instructor she ever had at UC. "What you jot down in a notebook in a college class is definitely different than having 80 little eyes looking at you when it's time to teach," McGuire said. "I've learned what children are interested in, how to catch their attention, and how to avoid some flops. I've helped set up this classroom; I've worked on my lesson plans. I can't imagine going into teaching prior to this kind of experience. I would have been petrified. Now, I think it's going to be another day of school."

"You end up with a better prepared teacher," agreed Armstrong, a 20-year elementary school teacher who likes teaching pupils from her rocking chair, where they gather around her. Her advice to McGuire ranged from tips on why to use big paper for spelling lists to critiques of lesson plans, asking McGuire to spell out not just which state standards her lessons cover but, more importantly, her own standards of what she expects children to learn from her teaching. "College alone does not prepare you for what really is out there in the real world," Armstrong said.

The real world, of course, has its way of complicating all manner of straightforward plans. And district finances created the biggest threats to establishing the Cincinnati partnership. Three years after it began, the program faced severe budget cuts by the district. This crisis looked like it was going to short-circuit the program until the university pledged $150,000 to keep the effort running for another year. Tight budgets have reappeared as a complicating factor throughout the program's history, forcing the union to fight just to keep the program going, leaving little time and energy to contemplate improvements or expansions. The financial stability of the program remained a question at the end of the 1990s.

Beyond its budget line, backers of the program adjusted the way they opened slots to serve UC students during a time when Cincinnati schools ordered districtwide layoffs. CFT officials had provided in their contract that the professional practice schools could not capture any vacancies created by teacher cutbacks. Financial pressures took a toll on how interns were assigned and paid. After budget cuts, only 18 captured positions remained in the fall of 1999 at the participating schools even though 90 interns were assigned, leaving a stipend of about $4,900 for each half-time teaching intern. That math also created more internship positions than supervisors, meaning that some interns in what the district calls "load-bearing" slots—where two students essentially cover a class—worked without a full-time teaching coach.

The budget woes also restricted the extent to which the district could make good on the ultimate goal of the program: getting more well-prepared new teachers into the district's classrooms. In recent years, job cuts meant that laid-off, or "surplus," teachers had rights to any openings. University of Cincinnati teaching students groomed in the partnership weren't candidates until final hirings were made in the late summer, only weeks before school opened. By then, many young candidates had gone to other districts. Some improvement came when a change in union policies allowed top-rated interns to be considered in the early rounds of placing surplus teachers. The chief players in the program said they found a way to cope with the budget problems and other obstacles, such as resistance to college professors' being asked to make connections with local schools. "Conceptualizing a true partnership is vastly different than implementing a true partnership," said Louis Castenell, dean of the education school at Cincinnati from 1990 to 1999, when he moved to a comparable job at the University of Georgia in Athens.

Beyond finances, organizers have found it difficult to recruit new schools to join the program. As a result, the university considered starting partnerships with suburban schools to create more slots. Some Cincinnati school administrators said the number of professional development schools did not grow because schools were under pressure to adopt other reforms that made principals and teachers reluctant to take on even more responsibilities. Indeed, the district was working to merge its elementary and middle schools into kindergarten-through-eighth-grade groups to create more academic continuity for adolescent pupils. School decision-making initiatives and other reform models also competed for educators' attention.

District officials, however, argued that schools were not avoiding the professional practice school model because of reform overload. Rather, they said, many educators were not interested in projects aimed at upgrading standards and the practices of teachers. "This is a tremendous task, and you don't just find people willing to take it on," said Kathleen Ware, an associate superintendent in Cincinnati and the district's chief representative in the college–school–union partnership. "We need to work more on the incentive side because improving teaching is something that interests some teachers but doesn't seem to interest a lot of teachers. I would have thought this would have spread much more quickly than it has."

Nationally, proponents of overhauling teacher education along the lines of the Cincinnati model have also been discouraged with the pace of change. A 1995 report from the Holmes Group, now known as the Holmes Partnership, sounded such a disappointed note. "Action must replace inertia," stated the group's report, *Tomorrow's Schools of Education*. "The education school should cease to act as a silent agent in the preservation of the status quo." The report added that if universities are unwilling to make connections with schools and boost the quality of their teacher-training programs, they should stop offering education degrees.

The Vicissitudes of Professional Development

Sue Taylor is well acquainted with bad public school teaching. And she has seen the price students and school systems pay for mediocrity and inadequacy. As a peer evaluator for the Cincinnati Federation of Teachers for 3 years, she witnessed the shortcomings of many teachers. "I was appalled by some of the practices and lack of knowledge I saw, and I wondered how some people made it through teacher education and certification," she said. "I thought every teacher had high expectations, knew content, and was able to motivate students, then I found some teachers who were working at the blackboard while their students were dancing in the back of the classroom."

Taylor worked through most of the 1990s to create the opposite kind of teacher as the professional development school coordinator at Hughes Center High. The experience gave her a sense of professional optimism at a time when she badly needed it, she said. She helped write college courses and even taught an introductory teaching course at UC. But while her involvement has offered some encouragement, it has also helped her realize the challenges the partnership still faces. While national groups plead for more colleges to involve themselves in stronger teacher training, Cincinnati was at a completely different crossroads after its 10-year effort, confronting how to make an innovative model program sustain itself and wondering whether it would ever grow beyond a limited-scale experiment. "The next step will be to make this program independent of the people who are doing the work now," said Lea Brinker, a lead teacher and coordinator at Western Hills High School.

Having navigated significant budget turmoil, the program faced a transition in leadership by the 1999–2000 academic year. Some people wondered how the partnership would fare under new Cincinnati superintendent Steven Adamowski. Sustaining momentum under different leadership first became a challenge with the departures of Yinger and Castenell from the university. In their absence, some school officials said they had witnessed less resolve from the college administrators and faculty to leave the comforts of academia to connect with schools. It showed up in various ways, large and small. Taylor was dropped as a teaching instructor at the college in favor of professors on the UC faculty. Heather McGuire, the Hays Elementary intern, and a fellow teaching intern at the school scrambled to find a video recorder to tape themselves teaching because the faculty member in charge of their class did not plan to visit the school to watch them in person.

Beyond questions about the impact of changes in leadership in the school district and at the university, some organizers said the Cincinnati partnership had yet to produce some of the intended effects of the professional development school model. Most notably, connections between schoolteachers and college faculty were scarce, since most of the interaction between the university and local schools occurred indirectly through the teaching students who move between the two realms. Discussions in schools between college professors and veteran teachers occurred infrequently. And research in school buildings akin to the work of teaching hospitals was almost nonexistent. "Part of the point was to connect two communities of researchers and practitioners who, in most of the country, exist in different worlds," said Tom Mooney of the Cincinnati teachers' union.

Meanwhile, as Cincinnati confronted the growing pains that came with maturity, the verdict was very much out on what would become of the larger effort to enhance teacher education by connecting schools and colleges. Some states were considering requirements that would force colleges to link up with schools, and the National Commission on the Accreditation of Teacher Education was on the verge of ratifying new standards that would require colleges to have partnerships with schools to meet accreditation requirements beginning in 2001. The push for professional development schools created models in some parts of the country that hardly embodied the serious connections envisioned by groups such as the Holmes Partnership or even the work in Cincinnati. For that reason, the national accrediting commission was also drafting new standards for those collaborations, offering guidelines and a seal of approval.

The effects of the collaboration in Cincinnati and similar ones elsewhere were summarized well by Jon Snyder, a senior researcher for the National Commission on Teaching and America's Future and director of teacher education at the University of California–Santa Barbara. After studying Cincinnati's teacher-training partnership and others across the country, he observed that even years into the program—and after a succession of awards and publicity about Cincinnati's trail-blazing work—continuing commitment from the university, district, and union remains a vital component if success is to be realized. "This requires institutional changes in districts, in schools, in classrooms, in higher education administration, in higher education faculty, and in unions. That's pretty much the whole universe," Snyder said. "I distrust anybody who says they can change the world without realizing how hard changing the world is. This program has been pretty honest about it."

CHAPTER 10

JACKSON STATE'S EFFORT TO HELP TEACHERS IN MISSISSIPPI

Monique Fields

A history of paying one of the lowest average teacher salaries in the nation. A new technology driving a thirst for knowledge. A federal mandate aimed at educating those who teach the youngest students. An educational work force aging so quickly that if all the teachers eligible to retire did so, more than 4,000 new teachers would be needed, almost three times the number who graduate each year. For Mississippi's elementary and secondary schools, these facts have led to the biggest effort at professional development for teachers that the state has seen in years. The programs, many of them located on college campuses, address almost every educator from Head Start personnel, to first-year educators, to master teachers. All of this means, for many teachers, that more training may lead to more money and, ultimately, a better education for the state's children.

In an effort that has other states taking note, the Mississippi Department of Education, federal governmental agencies, and colleges and universities across the state in the 1990s collaborated to ratchet up professional training. Together, they developed a myriad of programs, many facilitated through state-supported colleges and universities, institutions that long lived in a world isolated from elementary and secondary schools. Jackson State University, a historically Black college, is typical of the at least 10 higher education institutions throughout the state offering programs to teachers. Its three most developed programs focused on the professional development effort:

- To suit the master teacher, Jackson State opened its Southwest Mississippi World-Class Teaching Initiative, a mentoring program to pair teachers certified by the National Board for Professional Teaching Standards with those striving for this professional benchmark.
- For veteran teachers as well as beginning teachers, there was the Southwest Mississippi Education Consortium, to provide training for teachers who want to polish old skills or develop new ones.
- The Institute for Child Life Assessment, Studies and Services was developed to offer training to Head Start personnel, who face a federal mandate that 50% of them must have at least an associate degree in early childhood education by 2003.

All three programs were housed in the Institute for Educational Renewal, tucked away in Ayer Hall, the oldest building at Jackson State. "It is time to reach out. It's fine for us to sit up here and educate this unique group of students," said Johnnie Mills-Jones, director of the institute, "but just walk outside of that gate. There are all kinds of people who want help, but they don't know how to get it."

The state department of education did not have the money, the personnel, or the wherewithal to manage teacher-training programs, pushing the trend for colleges and universities such as Jackson State to do more to take it upon themselves to help teachers. The department used federal and state funds to contract with state-supported institutions. The program pumped money—albeit a small amount—into Jackson State. The Institute for Educational Renewal funded all three of its programs, excluding in-kind university contributions, such as facilities and telephone service, at a level of about $667,000 annually. Indeed, a different kind of education was blooming in Mississippi at the end of the 1990s. It was no longer acceptable to tell Johnny to pull out his book and read. He and his peers had to be engaged, and his teachers had to know how to hold the attention of their students. Some teachers lagged in this respect even before they picked up their first piece of chalk. They graduated from college with knowledge of educational theories, but not the practical experience needed in today's classroom. Complicating the issue were demands for accountability. Since teachers were held responsible for what their students did and did not learn, it forced them to seek the training to do the job better.

Teacher pay lies at the heart of the professional development issue. The expectations for teachers have risen, but in many states the salaries haven't kept pace. As a result, states such as Mississippi find their best and brightest talent turning their backs on the profession or seeking teaching jobs outside of the state. "I've seen a lot of teachers leave the classroom because they couldn't afford to be in the profession," said Marilyn Lowe, a lead teacher at Galloway Elementary School in Jackson. The state has long had low pay for teachers, ranking 49th out of 50 states. Mississippi public school teacher salaries averaged $29,530 in 1998–1999 compared with the national average of $40,582, according to the National Education Association. Connecticut and New Jersey topped the list, paying their teachers an average salary of more than $50,000 a year.

At least one of the programs housed at Jackson State may help move some Mississippi teachers closer to the nation's average teacher pay. Those teachers who complete a 1-year process and are able to earn National Board certification will be rewarded with an annual raise of $6,000 by the state for up to 10 years, the life of the certificate. The state also reimburses each candidate $2,000 for the cost of the application. It is all part of Mississippi's push to get more teachers certified by the National Board for Professional Teaching Standards. The certificate is so prestigious that about 20 states accept national certification in lieu of passing state teaching licensure exams. Teachers spend about 200 hours working on a portfolio that details their teaching philosophy, student work, and lesson plans. A set of written examinations focuses on content knowledge as well as pedagogy.

"It really affirmed that I was doing what I needed to be doing with my life. The decision I made when I was 20 was the right one," said Lowe, who received National Board certification in 1998. The Jackson State program will follow teachers through the entire process, coaching them on the preparation of their portfolios. Thus far, programs similar to Jackson State's have been successful at other Mississippi colleges, giving the state 354 National Board–certified teachers. In 1995, only 9% of those taking the examination actually passed it. A year later, Mississippi State University opened the state's first mentoring program. Most recently, the number attempting the test and passing it rose to 49%, the same as the national rate.

Other challenges remain. About 700 Mississippi teachers applied for certification in 1999, boosting the amount of money needed to pay those who pass the test. "They have offered this carrot for teachers. What's going to happen when we have 1,000 board-certified teachers? Is the money still going to be there?" asked Leslie Coleman, director of the teaching initiative at Jackson State, who received National Board certification in 1999. At the same time, some Mississippi teachers wonder why they have to prove themselves to get a raise, which, in many cases, will still leave their salaries below national averages. It is likely the money will be there. "I tell them not to fight the system," said Peggy Swoger, director of the World-Class Teaching Program at Mississippi State University and a founding member of the National Board. "If they want a pay raise, this is the way to go."

Jackson State also must wrestle with its duplication of an existing mentoring program in the Jackson public schools to help prepare teachers for National Board certification. Each year since 1997, 25 Jackson teachers have been able to turn to their own district for help. Jackson is the largest school district in the state and needs to provide opportunities for all potential candidates, Lowe said. Teachers benefit from on-site assistance with their portfolio, as well as access to electronic equipment needed to complete the process. On the other hand, Jackson State draws most of its candidates from outside the city. Lowe and Coleman said the programs don't compete. But some Jackson schoolteachers applied for both. Since Jackson State plans to expand beyond its 50 slots, it is likely to threaten and possibly force an end to the Jackson public schools' mentoring program.

As Jackson State fields its first class of protégés seeking National Board certification, it cannot escape the race issue. The Mississippi state program and others like it across the state fall short when it comes to the number of minority teachers seeking and qualifying for National Board certification. Of the 354 teachers already certified in Mississippi, only 2 are African American. It is unclear how many African American teachers have tried and failed, or why more African American teachers haven't attempted certification. The issue may be rooted in fear of failure. Other, more complex reasons elude researchers. "In working with them, some of them have a very difficult time getting their teaching down on paper," Swoger said. Jackson State, which plans to mirror Mississippi State's certification success, has enrolled 50 teachers in its mentoring program. Coleman, the director of the program, plans to go one step further and ensure that the program produces certified Black candidates as well. Of the 50 teachers enrolled in Jackson State's program, 35% are African American.

Using the National Board as a means to give teachers merit raises is a safe venture. The state doesn't have to decide who receives the bonus. Furthermore, achieving National Board certification is strictly voluntary, virtually taking politics out of the picture. As a result, programs such as the one at Jackson State have received bipartisan support. The National Board has taken note, using Mississippi as a model for other states, including Oklahoma. North Carolina leads the nation with 1,262 National Board—certified teachers and credits this success, in part, to having produced an upswing in national achievement test scores by public schools throughout the state. Mississippi stands fourth in the number of teachers who have earned National Board certification. In 1999, the National Board certified 2,965 teachers, raising the total of board-certified teachers throughout the country to 4,799. Mississippi was also among 31 states offering multiple incentives to recruit candidates for certification, providing financial support to them if they pass, and using the certification as a means to distinguish teachers. Of course, officials in Mississippi hope that the long-term effect of all this will rub off on the state's schoolchildren and raise their achievement levels as a result of the instruction that they receive.

Assistance for the Other Teachers

Still, the work with the National Board has addressed only part of the professional development issue. For seasoned and beginning teachers, Jackson State developed a program, the Southwest Mississippi Education Consortium, to help teachers after they left the college classroom and entered their own classrooms as teachers. This was one of the programs that contracted with the department of education, after the state realized it didn't have the personnel to deliver teacher training on its own. Colleges and universities, including Jackson State, picked up the baton and the federal and state funds that came with the program, delivering technology training, teaching instruction, and other needs identified by local school districts.

Angela Snellgrove instructs 18 children every day, but she doesn't have all the techniques and personal tools she needs to deliver the education they need. The third-grade teacher at Mendenhall Elementary School in Simpson County, about 35 miles outside of Jackson, is doing something about it, one click at a time. Recently she took a class through the Consortium to help her better understand computers and how they can be integrated into the classroom. A month after taking the class, she walked her students through a graphing lesson. Four out of five of Snellgrove's students have access to computers at home, but a few months ago she rarely used one in her classroom.

Still a novice herself, she found the lesson to be a series of starts and restarts as she guessed her way through a maze of computer screens a few days before Thanksgiving. Snellgrove clutched an instruction book for Microsoft Works 3.0 as she took her students through the more advanced 4.0 program installed on her computer. "Our only problem doing this is the instructions," said Snellgrove, who had been teaching 3 years. "The directions are slightly different." When complete, the bar chart clearly showed that turkey and pumpkin pie are far more popular than dressing. "I wanted them to understand it, to see the math, to see how important it is to them," she said. The graphing lesson illustrated and reinforced what the children already knew. Their mothers and fathers preferred their turkey without the dry dressing.

Jackson State brought the technology workshop to the Mendenhall schools on a scheduled teacher in-service day and provided a training opportunity that might otherwise have gone unused in rural Simpson County with its seven schools. In order to train all the county's teachers, principals would first have to select candidates, hire substitutes to teach their classes, and then pay for their training. Otherwise, the burden would be left on the teachers' shoulders. "Teachers know that there are weak areas. It doesn't necessarily mean they will go and do extra work. It takes money and time," said Onnie Lee, principal of Mendenhall Junior High School.

Teachers earned much-needed continuing education units through Jackson State's program, but it was not a cure-all for what ailed Mississippi schools and their teachers. Kathryn Jones, a language arts and special education teacher at Mendenhall Junior High School, attended the same technology workshop as Snellgrove. She had yet to incorporate the computer into her lessons. "I have one computer in my class on the Internet," Jones said. "If you have 10 or 11 kids in your class, you can't get to the computer in 55 minutes." She does work on it in her free time, which she has more of this year than last year. "It just sat there," she said. It was unclear where she would find the time, but Jones planned to use the computer to post grades and teach graphs.

Of the three programs offered by Jackson State's Institute for Education Renewal, it was the Southwest Mississippi Education Consortium that garnered the most participation from Jackson State faculty. Still, it was difficult to recruit professors, given their workloads and a modest stipend of only $100 to $200 for their expertise. Locord D. Wilson, an assistant professor and a technical assistant for the Consortium at Jackson State, did not lend her expertise for the money. "If we go in there and assist, we are telling them what we're looking for, what kind of student we at Jackson State want and need," she said. The training work was often viewed as extra work and was seen as time-consuming. The larger issue, of course, was the connection between college and classroom; not only the schools reap benefits from such an alliance. The college gains, too, as it reestablishes itself with the teaching community, possibly quelling criticism that many of its professors have not seen the inside of a traditional classroom in decades.

The Consortium's courses were aimed at helping beginning teachers and veteran professionals better educate their students. One such person, Johnnie Johnson, a first-year teacher at Jefferson County Elementary, was pursuing her second career. She was a graduate of Alcorn State University with a master's degree in special education, but she was surprised by her lack of preparation. She walked into the classroom "not knowing what to expect or how to proceed." Her students suffered from boredom, until she attended a workshop coordinated by Jackson State. It gave her the tools she needed to integrate curriculum in her classroom. She said: "When we're reading stories, I can point out to them capitalization. It helps with their memory. When we're constantly going over a subject, it will stay with them longer." Like her students, Johnson yearned for more knowledge and signed up for two additional workshops to better equip her for the classroom.

A training session for administrators illustrated the hefty challenge confronting the Consortium. On the last day of a 10-day class, 20 assistant principals, principals, and superintendents tweaked Power Point demonstrations about the Internet and its use in the classroom at Enterprise School, a rural K–12 school in Brookhaven, 50 miles south of Jackson. What was clear from the beginning was that the teachers-turned-administrators knew very little about computers before taking the class. They were overwhelmed by the technology and used it like children who had just learned something new. They saturated their presentations with sounds and visuals. It was practical experience all of them needed in order to do their jobs better. Many of them knew only how to turn the machines on and off, and some of them acted as if they feared the mouse might bite them. After a while, however, the administrators learned how to navigate the Internet, monitor children's Web-based activities, and deliver a PowerPoint presentation. Leroy Kelly, Jr., the principal at Port Gibson High School, had been evaluating computer classes with no concrete knowledge. "I had no clue what they were doing," he said, referring to computer technology teachers and their students. "Now, I can tell if they are on task or playing games." The Consortium often developed programs specifically to fit a school's needs. Weeks before the program, teachers completed needs-assessment sheets, setting priorities for what they deemed most important to learn. Principals tallied the surveys.

Despite the need for the program, the Consortium canceled some courses for lack of participation, a signal that more had to be done to inform teachers and principals of the existence of the classes, which were free. Program administrators also continued to struggle with getting school districts to understand that teachers and principals needed to attend workshops together to make the learning most successful for the school. Teachers complained that they did not know the program existed or how it could help them. Many of them did not know the courses were organized by Jackson State. Some of those who did know about Jackson State's involvement viewed the historically Black school as inferior and far less organized than the state's predominately White institutions, which had a similar training program for teachers. Such are the impediments to school–college collaboration.

Worst of all, there was little or no information to indicate that the program actually worked. In its first 3 years, the Consortium hadn't been formally evaluated by the Mississippi Department of Education. The first year was merely a pilot program. In the second year, the state education department got a new superintendent. Another year passed as the state decided to evaluate students using different measurements. By its fourth year, in 1999–2000, the effects of the program on quality teaching, if any, were still not known.

The Third Piece: Helping Head Start Teachers

A third professional development program for teachers aimed to help Head Start teachers gain respect and, more importantly, better prepare their students for kindergarten and first grade. The Institute for Child Life Assessment, Studies and Services, or I-CLASS, addressed that issue, training Head Start teachers and teacher's assistants, who are responsible for 25,000 children in Mississippi. Jackson State and Head Start began working together in 1998.

Each year until 2001, Jackson State and four other historically Black colleges in Mississippi were to receive a total of $125,000 from the U.S. Department of Health and Human Services. The collaboration was spearheaded by Jackson State and aimed to train Head Start employees in the state's 82 counties. Until 1992, Head Start personnel were required to complete only 120 hours of informal training and received a Child Development Association endorsement, or CDA, certification. Driven by the need to educate teachers who teach the nation's youngest students, the federal government mandated in 1998 that 50% of Head Start teachers must have at least an associate degree by 2003. It was an effort to reinvent Head Start, stabilize the early childhood work force, increase pay, and establish a career ladder for upwardly mobile teachers. "They cannot prepare children for the first grade if they are not prepared," said Mary Daniel, director of I-CLASS.

Head Start teachers and teacher's assistants could lose their jobs if they didn't comply. To meet the new requirement, Head Start personnel had to overcome intimidation, long-distance van rides, and weary days. They had to learn about the stages of development and brain development in infants and toddlers. Jackson State tried to facilitate this process. Professors packed up their teaching wares and hauled them to rural counties, as far as 160 miles from Jackson State. Head Start paid the tuition costs. The instruction was helping some. A typical student such as Barbara Peters, a Head Start teacher in Kokomo, wasn't sure why a 5-year-old boy was unable to hold a pencil or complete a three-piece puzzle. But, with help, she learned to teach such a child and credited her newfound teaching abilities to lessons she learned in the classroom. "I think the problem was me a little bit," she said. "I learned to step back and let the child be more free to do whatever he thinks is best."

Many of the people who work for Head Start have done so for their entire careers and will do almost anything to protect their jobs. Mae Foxworth, a teacher's assistant at Lexie Head Start in Tylertown, was "intimidated because of my age" when she went back to college in January 1998. The 50-year-old woman sat next to students who were younger than her three grown children. She hadn't been on a campus in more than 15 years. Intimidation soon turned to frustration. Her days were filled with helping children learn the alphabet, and then she had to spend 2 nights a week pushing a pencil in 3-hour classes. Summers were the worst. During the school year, the programs were offered at Head Start centers. But in the summer, teachers had to board a free van to go to Jackson State for math, biology, and computer courses. Foxworth's ritual began at 5:45 A.M., when she met colleagues in a grocery store parking lot every day for the 2-hour drive north from McComb to Jackson. Her days ended after 7 P.M. "The hardest part about it was the ride," Foxworth said. "It just wore you out every day for 2 months." She called it a "sacrifice."

It was a sacrifice for the professors as well, because of the need to rely heavily on adjunct professors, instead of full-time faculty, many of whom declined to be involved. Concerns arose when students had questions about whether they would be able to contact peripatetic adjunct professors. Peggy Answorth, director of the Pinebelt Association for Community Enhancement Inc. in Hattiesburg, was one of those adjunct professors. She received a doctoral degree in early childhood education from Jackson State in 1996, but she had been teaching at the college level for only about a year. Two days a week, she drove 2 hours to lead two classes for 30 women. She signed up to teach one class, but the shortage of professors forced her to teach twice a week. It was stressful. "I think about the end results," she said. "The end translates into a better Head Start program. I'm going to do it as long as I am able to."

Compounding the issue was the fact that many of the Head Start people had not been students for many years. They arrived with deficiencies that had to be addressed before enrollment in their first college course. "If you go on campus, you don't get a pep talk. You don't get somebody to listen to your personal problems," Answorth said.

THERE WAS NO clear cut way to evaluate the impact of Jackson State's professional development efforts and their effect on teacher quality. The best evidence was anecdotal. And in all three programs, the key to success hinged, in some part, on how many full-time college professors lent their time and expertise to them. Faculty participation was scant, because there weren't any real incentives for professors. Future success would be determined by how many of them bought into the program.

Still, other states and institutions of higher learning could learn from Mississippi's mistakes and triumphs. The Southwest Mississippi World-Class Teaching Initiative, a mentoring program for teachers attempting to become certified by the National Board for Professional Teaching Standards, was set to be the most successful. There was no doubt that Mississippi and the incentives it used to lure teachers would boost the state's average teacher salaries. In 1999, Mississippi had the fourth-largest number of National Board–certified teachers, dwarfing some of its border states, such as Tennessee, that had few incentives and support mechanisms in place. Unfortunately, a gulf existed between the number of White teachers and Black teachers who had received the certification. Mississippi was playing catch-up and tried to spark more interest among African American teachers. Programs at colleges across the state hadn't quite figured out how to reach African American teachers, but administrators planned to used the few who had achieved National Board certification as mentors to help bring up the ranks in 2000.

The Southwest Mississippi Education Consortium provided training for teachers who wanted to sharpen their teaching acumen or build new skills. It marked its success in the number of people trained, but the training could prove useless in just a few years, especially if the learning stopped there. Mississippi Department of Education administrators realized they had to reach beyond their bureaucratic comfort zones and work with institutions charged with making their state a better place. But it took 4 years for the state and its institutions of higher education to realize that the best results from professional development programs could be attained when they were evaluated on an annual basis. Such evaluations would prove necessary in order to strengthen those programs. The state Department of Education planned to evaluate professional teaching development coordinated at institutions such as Jackson State for the first time in 2000.

With the help of the Institute for Child Life Assessment, Studies and Services and Mississippi's historically Black colleges, the state could meet a federal mandate that 50% of Head Start personnel have at least an associate degree in early childhood education by 2003. But in their quest to educate Head Start personnel, the schools and Head Start agencies placed a heavy burden on those seeking education. This could lead to the detriment of the program if only the willfully determined make the almost daily sacrifices needed to complete requirements for the associate degree. Mississippi got a jump start on the mandate, beginning its program with historically Black colleges in 1996. Those extra years could help it become one of the states that meets the mandate in 2003. Still, Jackson State and the other Black colleges served only a small number of students in 1999. The university needed somehow to motivate more faculty to participate, as well as to get the message to Head Start personnel and find additional dollars to run the programs. Otherwise, some Head Start agencies could be in a state of confusion in 2003 and not have enough personnel to meet the classroom requirement the state's youngest students need the most: qualified teachers.

PART V

Community Building

Mention of town and gown crops up frequently in higher education. And, all too often, the phrase evokes negative stereotypes. It wasn't by accident that colleges and universities were called "ivory towers." Yet, in some notable instances, academics have descended from the towers, rolled up their sleeves, and gotten involved in their communities. On these occasions, the contributions of higher education have helped revivify neighborhoods and improve elementary and secondary schools. Some of those institutions most willing to take these steps have done so for reasons that combine altruism and self-interest. Other colleges and universities, feeling no such imperative, have remained aloof from their surroundings, giving no more than lip service to the role that they might play in community building.

One of the longest-lasting and most ambitious of the collaboratives involves the University of Pennsylvania and the low-income West Philadelphia neighborhood in which it is situated. Penn's experience contains lessons for other institutions that would like to win acceptance from neighbors who initially regard the university with well-founded suspicion. One of the Penn administrators interviewed by Dale Mezzacappa told her that "any university considering such a move must carefully consider its intent." He said that university faculty must see value in getting involved and not regard it as a one-way street in which they conduct research and then leave. On the other hand, according to Mezzacappa, the elementary and secondary schools in the neighborhood must be willing to put what may have been a bad relationship with the university behind them and start anew.

In Hartford, Connecticut, Trinity University, like Penn, faced a future in a neighborhood that was crumbling at the very doorstep of the university. And, like Penn, Trinity took giant steps to help its community rebuild. Says Rick Green: "Trinity discovered that by aggressively taking the lead—and pumping its human resources and $6 million from its own endowment into the project—a small, wealthy institution can be a powerful redevelopment force."

Both case studies are works-in-progress, affirming positive possibilities but also remaining fragile and subject to setbacks. What is clear in these two instances is that a university is unlikely to be able to intervene, make a quick fix, and leave, expecting that everything will be fine in the community. In fact, Penn and Trinity show that well-meaning institutions of higher education must build permanent collaborations with their neighbors if they hope to make a difference in the long run. This will not be easy.

CHAPTER 11

PENN AND WEST PHILADELPHIA

Dale Mezzacappa

May 13, 1985, was one of the most tragic days in the history of Philadelphia. In an effort to dislodge the troublesome back-to-nature group MOVE, the police department bombed its row house, inadvertently setting off a fire that engulfed two city blocks, displaced 53 families, and killed 11 people. It's hard to imagine that anything good could come out of an event like this, but it did. The MOVE fire served as the catalyst that propelled the fledgling West Philadelphia Improvement Corps into what is now one of the most far-reaching collaborations between an urban university and the schools in its surrounding neighborhood.

That spring, American history professor Lee Benson and one of his former students, Ira Harkavy, were running a seminar at the University of Pennsylvania campus for about 20 students called "University and Community Relations: Penn–West Philadelphia, Past, Present, and Future." The history was not pretty, with Penn gobbling up entire city blocks for its own expansion, often destroying stable, mostly African American neighborhoods in the process. In the beginning, Harkavy, then a Penn administrator, and Benson merely wanted to find ways to improve the relationship between Penn and the distressed urban neighborhood that surrounds it. For that summer, they had the modest goal of establishing a youth corps with 50 area teens to work with Penn students on beautification and cleanup projects. They had a small $20,000 grant from United Parcel Service—and the indifference or outright suspicions of city agencies with the power to kick in additional funds.

But after the MOVE tragedy, "we got big-scale money from the city, and we relocated the entire project to the MOVE neighborhood," Harkavy recalled. Sixty teenagers affected by MOVE worked all summer around a neighborhood recreation center and school, painting a mural, cleaning up the trash-strewn grass, and planting trees. Sheldon Hackney, then the president of the university, authorized funds for a landscape architect to work on the project. Suddenly, the city and the university were both heavily involved in Harkavy and Benson's dream. And something magical began happening, especially at the Bryant School, located about a mile from the university campus. Neighbors—senior citizens, mostly—donated lawn mowers and garden tools, and worked side by side with the teens and Penn students. Teachers gave up their time to lend a hand. As the new community of workers hauled away the broken glass and other detritus of decline, the beaten-down grass came to life. As the residents, teenagers, and Penn students painstakingly applied paint to the dank brick, the school itself took on a whole new aura. And, for Harkavy, the possibilities suddenly became clear. His and Benson's nascent ideas began to evolve into something much more focused and far more ambitious.

Fired by the theories of John Dewey on problem-based learning and fascinated by their research into the history of the community schools movement, Benson and Harkavy saw no end to the possibilities: They would create community schools in their urban neighborhood and challenge the very assumptions underlying the university's purpose. "We realized the best way Penn could do something constructive in West Philadelphia was through public schools," said Benson, now an emeritus history professor. "When we started, we didn't know anything about John Dewey. The basic argument we made then and continue to make now is that only if the school system improves can West Philadelphia and the neighborhood improve."

As an undergraduate at Penn in the 1960s, Harkavy had led protests against both the university's destructive expansion and its involvement in Vietnam-related military research. He talks fast, and his thoughts often trip over each other, but this makes his ever-growing excitement a palpable force. "That summer," he said, "we saw a result. We had a sense that schools could be neighborhood centers. The idea of learning by community problem solving, the idea of the problems of the community being the curriculum of the school . . . it all came together." Not immediately. But eventually. Today, nearly 15 years later, Harkavy and Benson still teach that seminar. But, in addition, there are fully 96 courses offered at Penn, distributed over nearly all the 12 schools at the university, in which students do some of their work and research in the community.

The founders of what has come to be known as the Center for Community Partnerships have nothing less in mind than redefining the role of the university and remaking K–12 education. They believe it's a matter of mutual survival. As Harkavy and Benson wrote in 1993, "Unless our public school system is radically transformed, the crisis in cities and society will only get worse and universities will suffer for it." Not to mention that the historic mission of the university is to create a better society, not simply to advance some abstract concept of learning. Or, as Harkavy put it more bluntly, "universities cannot afford to remain shores of affluence, self-importance, and horticultural beauty at the edge of island seas of squalor, violence, and despair."

MALEEKA BORDERS, 8, stood inside the front door of the Drew Elementary School, three blocks from the Penn campus, on the first cold day of winter in 1999. School was over, but not for Maleeka. She was selling fruits and vegetables from a stand. Wadin McKie, 12, bought a bag of grapes and handed Maleeka a dollar bill. The third grader, nearly obscured by the piles of grapes, bananas, grapefruit, apples, and asparagus in front of her, carefully counted out Wadin's change: three quarters. Tamara Dubowitz and Dan Gerbner, Penn graduate students in anthropology under Professor Frank Johnston, were supervising this enterprise. A few minutes later, they checked the foot traffic and decided it was trailing off. "Time to pack up," Dubowitz said. The Drew students eagerly plunged into the task, gathering up their unsold wares and dismantling the jigsaw-like table they had designed themselves.

Right about that time, Makeeka's classmate Quideea James, 8, was hunched over a book in the school library downstairs. "I looked for more bugs in the mud," she read, watched over by Penn senior Carrie Pierce and surrounded by a few dozen other students and their tutors. "I found a bad red bug in the mud." The next sentence had a word that totally stumped Quideea—"Todd." She kept saying, "Ty." Pierce kept urging, "Sound it out, sound it out, look at the letters." Quideea eventually did, getting the word right, but it was a struggle. Pierce was a student in Professor William Labov's linguistic class, "Introduction to African American English." After attending a class session, she and the other students went to Drew to tutor and test out new approaches for teaching young children to read. Labov, with several collaborators, wrote the manual Quideea was using, unusual in that it incorporates the cadences and rhyming patterns of hip-hop. It's an effort to help solve the enduring challenge of teaching inner-city Black students to read well.

Johnston's nutrition work and Labov's linguistics research are examples of Harkavy and Benson's ideas come to fruition—more than service learning, more than tutoring, more than field work. West Philadelphia, in effect, has become a laboratory for these professors and their students to do pioneering research in their fields. "What's unique about our program is that the knowledge and information we're gaining is directly related to the problems we're trying to solve," Labov said. "We're not just taking what we know and using it in the community." So when Quideea stumbles over the word "Todd," Labov is gaining insight into how African American children connect letters to sounds. And he's trying to design a controlled study to see whether students using the reading book he and his colleagues have developed make more reading progress. "We know that the children are not looking at the alphabet in the same way," Labov said. "We know that these African American children have a spoken language that's much more different from the alphabet [than that of most children.]"

The two dozen Penn students in his course, all of whom tutor in the schools, bring him back useful information every day. "In a lot of service programs at universities, the students are just interested in helping," Labov said. "Here, we're making the connection between unsolved problems in linguistics and unsolved problems in teaching reading." The Penn students like it. "We should share what we learn with the rest of the community so they can be in the same spot we are in the future," said Pierce, an economics major from Long Island. Traci Curry, another Labov student who went through the public schools in Washington, D.C., said she was pleasantly surprised. "Unlike a whole lot of universities, Penn is right in the middle of city neighborhoods that are underserved in many ways," she said. "I'm glad to know the university has a commitment to work with and in the community."

Both Gerbner and Dubowitz began as undergraduates at Penn and have built their careers around their neighborhood research in the area of nutrition. "It's a classic story," said Dubowitz, whose field is applied medical anthropology. "In poorer neighborhoods, people make poorer food choices and have poorer access to healthy foods." Her specific interest is the higher prevalence in these neighborhoods of diet-related disease, including stroke, diabetes, and some cancers. At Drew, in addition to operating the stand, students grow their own foods and vegetables in a garden. She thinks her efforts are paying off. "One mother came up to me and said her daughter made her read all the food labels and we couldn't buy anything with high fat content," Dubowitz said, smiling.

Gerbner's interests are slightly different. After graduating from Penn, he taught in the public schools for a while. His interest is using this program to rebuild the curriculum. The students operating the fruit stand, for instance, learn a lot about math by making change and taking inventory. They learn about science through working in the garden. Dubowitz can't imagine doing the sort of isolated, ivory-tower research that can be typical at universities. The mutual benefits are apparent. "For me, I'd have a hard time doing it any other way," she said. Jacki Popielarski, a teacher at Drew who serves as a coordinator for the Penn programs there, presided over these after-school activities. "Penn helps us have a variety of programs we may not have had, at least not on this scale," she said. "The university is a major positive force for the kids." Drew showed more improvement between 1996 and 1999 in reading and math in fifth and eighth grades than any other school in the state in the Pennsylvania System of State Assessment tests, although there was no research to link the improvement specifically to Penn's involvement. Harkavy said he suspected that it was due to a number of factors, including a strong principal. "But the fact is," he said, "we're doing reading and nutrition at that school in a big way."

Spreading the Impact

Marie Bogle was one of the teachers who got involved in the summer project in 1985 at the Bryant Elementary School. At that point in her career, she was ready to give it all up. "I was one of those burned-out teachers," she said. "I was not happy about returning to work as a teacher. It offered me little fulfillment at that time." In the spring of 1985, she went in to talk to the principal, June Harrison Brown, about the next year's appointment, and by luck or fate, Harkavy phoned while she was in the principal's office. He was seeking a teacher to coordinate a more comprehensive, year-long program at Bryant that would deepen the work begun in the summer and turn Bryant into a true community school. Brown pointed to Bogle. "She'll do it," Brown told Harkavy. "Do what?" asked Bogle. When another teacher agreed to help out, Bogle found herself immersed in a project that would take up the better part of the next 15 years and rejuvenate her career.

Her reluctance was born not just of her frustration with a school system that bumped her from place to place and didn't offer support, but also from attitudes about the university. "Penn had a bad reputation," Bogle said. Even after the successful summer at Bryant, "I could see some resentment of these White kids coming into the community. Yet we had done something positive." By that time, Bogle was teaching special education students. Initially, she and the other teacher took their students out to maintain the mural and the landscaping, still casting about for how to expand the program. "I started teaching my children what a community was, what a neighbor was, and, after a while, they started knocking on doors and introducing themselves," she said.

The change in her students who engaged in this simple activity was, as she put it, miraculous. "They went home and told their parents what they were doing," Bogle said, "and that turned everything around for me, the tremendous parental support. I saw we *had* to do something different for the kids." Her students were both learning and engaged, and parents were proud of what their children were accomplishing. Before long, her students, some of whom were severely handicapped, were producing oral histories. Everything, suddenly, became a learning tool, even the calendar, and all this was shared with the neighbors and parents. Students made placemats for the families, painted numbers on their mailboxes. Gradually, the curriculum was built around the real world—and the students did better on tests than they had before. "We were just doing something that, I guess, made sense," Bogle said. "We weren't wasting time; kids were learning and we were still within policy. We felt we were doing something right, and it went from there." From that point, "learning by doing" became her credo.

Other principals became interested, especially Robert Chapman at Turner Middle School. As happens in school systems, principals come and go; when Brown left Bryant, support for Bogle's work dropped off. So in 1987 she went to Turner, "and it was a whole new ballgame." She created an after-school program for particularly troublesome kids, who cleaned up graffiti on the school grounds and then protected their work, rallying the neighbors in the process.

But the goal of the Penn sponsors was to create a true community school, one around which the neighborhood revolves. That's what they did at Turner, which gained a national reputation for its virtually round-the-clock operations and special programs. Not only could all members of the community take courses in subjects as varied as computers, airplane modeling, and vegetarian cooking on Saturdays, but eighth-graders who worked one morning a week at Penn's hospital taught evening classes in the neighborhood on hypertension and did some supervised initial screening. Residents also got a chance to teach courses in their areas of expertise. This was all in addition to cleanup and beautification projects, which continued. But not all the effects were on weekends and after school. "We really started to restructure schools through the philosophy that all kids could learn," said Bogle. "And we saw that we had to change the way in which we were teaching them to make education relevant."

There was still a lot of skepticism among other teachers that all the work would be worth it, accustomed as they were to institutions such as Penn giving one-shot grants and then moving on. And it wasn't always clear how Penn would help. But several teachers were willing to take the chance—spending a lot of time planning, getting involved in new kinds of schedules, scrapping old lessons. The key was getting students out into the communities to do research and work, even those who teachers may have thought weren't capable. And then the teachers had to figure out how to make sure students were learning the right math or science skills through the project. They did investigations of the nutritional habits of families through Johnston and his Penn students and had a fruit and vegetable store there, too. "When I left Turner this year, we had every teacher involved in this program," said Bogle. "But it was a hard struggle."

Gradually, the attitude of the neighborhood toward Penn changed; initially, Penn students found it unsettling to take the trolley to the neighborhood at night. Perhaps the most dramatic evidence of the turnaround in attitude was when the neighborhood dedicated a garden to the memory of a Penn student who was killed in an accident. In projects such as the one on nutrition, the community was an active partner, not simply a research subject.

"The Penn people they kept their word, that they were not just there to take something away and give their own students an 'experience'; they were there to give and to learn from this community, too," said Bogle. The two-way street operated in other ways, too. At least one young man from Turner was inspired to attend Penn as a result of his contact with students and the extra academic and social supports he received. David Rice is now a pre-med sophomore. "They made me see what I could aspire to," he said.

From Penn's Perspective

On the Penn side, not everyone was convinced that community-based activity was worthwhile. "Some professors doubted whether it's a way to advance their own work and the learning of their students," said Harkavy. "But once many of the faculty try it, they like it, but some say this is not what higher education does. But it is what higher education did in the past." In the eighteenth and nineteenth centuries, he said, the mission of the American university was not simply to advance learning but also to create a better society. Today, however, status within the university is often tied to arcane research. But gradually, more and more professors are finding it rewarding and beneficial to rethink their approach to their disciplines.

Peter Conn, an English professor, meets each spring with teachers from University City High School. Located just three blocks from Penn's campus, "Uni," as it is called, typifies all the struggles of urban high schools: a student body that is overwhelmingly poor, almost entirely minority—Black and Asian—and plagued with low test scores, high dropout rates, and problems with weapons and crime. Conn asks the teachers what books and curriculum plans they have for the next fall. Then he designs his American literature course around those texts, and his students serve as teaching assistants in the University City classrooms. "They do curriculum planning, find background material, work with small groups of kids," said James M. "Torch" Lytle, the former principal at University City and now the superintendent of schools in Trenton, New Jersey. "The undergraduates love it. It's intellectually stimulating for them and for him, plus it creates smaller class size and high-intensity instruction at the high school."

Before Lytle, who also teaches an urban education course at Penn's graduate school of education, arrived at "Uni," the relationship between the high school and the university was one of distrust. He worried especially about the "fishbowl" aspect: the notion that Penn researchers were using the high school for their own academic ends without really helping the students or teachers. "There have been instances where students or faculty members or parents have felt folks from Penn were not sufficiently respectful," Lytle said. In the past, the university had given grants that benefited researchers who spent a lot of time in the high school but had negligible benefits for the students there. "If the benefits for us weren't clear," he said, "we wouldn't get involved."

In one particularly successful program, Lytle said, special education students spend 1 day a week working in areas such as food service and maintenance at Penn, the largest private employer in Philadelphia. The community residents who work in these departments mentor them, and they often get hired when they graduate. A professor in the education school has documented the success of this approach to school-to-work for students who, traditionally, have been unemployable. "These are kids who have a negative sense of self and didn't even see themselves as working at McDonald's," said Lytle. On balance, he said, "the array of things that have emerged and continue to emerge is really remarkable."

Part of that is due to the hard work of Cory Bowman, a former student of Harkavy's. Since 1991, he has been the apostle of community-based learning at the university, helping professors craft new courses—even redirect their academic focus—and negotiating the participation of schools and community. When he started, there were 12 courses with a community focus; now, there are fully eight times that many. While many of the courses have focused on more the traditional subjects of arts and humanities and social work, the next big step, he said, is to get more that concentrate on math, science, and computers.

Dennis DeTurck, chairman of the math department, got a National Science Foundation grant through Bowman and Harkavy's center, in which graduate student fellows help teachers in West Philadelphia High School, about eight blocks west, with science and math curriculum ideas. One project is using Wisconsin "fast plants," which grow rapidly, for hands-on units on genetics. "The high school students can see the genetics happen," DeTurck said. "All the stuff I learned from reading a book, they can see it." On the other end, he said, "We're trying to impart the idea that caring about and being involved with K–12 education is part and parcel of what scientists do." In just half a year with this grant, "we've had some students decide that maybe what they really want to do is teach, and that would be great, if we could get more teachers who were trained in a serious way in science and math."

The partnerships touch nearly all aspects of the university. Ann Spirn in the Urban Studies Department works with teachers and students at Sulzberger Middle School to build community gardens, do land-use planning, and in-

vestigate the environment of Mill Creek. William Yalowitz, in Theater Arts Department, works with the Black Bottom Performance Project. People from the displaced sections of the Penn neighborhood, called the Black Bottom, work with students from the college and University City High to create theatrical productions about the very history that has caused so much tension. "It's definitely a reciprocal relationship," said Yalowitz. "My students benefit at least as much if not more than the students and teachers and community people we work with. It brings enormous vitality to learning that is sometimes happening in a vacuum." Plus, he said, it's the right thing to do. "This is primarily about the sharing of resources. The university represents a huge aggregation of resources that should be distributed with economic justice in mind."

Community groups by and large find the relationship with Penn productive. Frances Walker, a lifelong activist in the neighborhood and president of two community groups, said that the university has learned the value of partnership. She cited Ann Spirn's project at Sulzberger Middle School on Mill Creek, a neighborhood waterway that has caused sinking, shifting homes and other environmental problems. The Sulzberger students are learning science by studying the creek, and, in turn, they educate their parents and neighbors. Spirn also teaches classes for adults on Saturdays to help them identify whether plumbing and water problems in their homes may be related to the creek.

"She's been working with us for 12 years," Walker said of Spirn. "Gaining these kinds of resources is invaluable to the community." Most important, she said, "We create the programs together. They don't come in here and say, 'We're going to put this program in your community.' We work together on the priorities of the community rather than people just doing things they think we need." Besides that, Penn has helped nonprofit organizations such as Spirn's Parents and Children Against Drugs, with training, accounting, and grant applications. When the air-conditioning broke down in the old building in which the organization is based, the Engineering Department at the university even helped get the system repaired. Walker, now 65, began protesting against Penn's actions when she was just 14 years old. She and her girlfriends objected at that time to prohibitions that kept them from walking on campus. "You can never completely make up for the past," she said, "but I've seen a remarkable change in their efforts to work with the community."

Penn's involvement in trying to improve public education in Philadelphia is not limited to Harkavy's partnership. Thirteen years ago, Penn alumnus and philanthropist George Weiss established the Say Yes to Education Foundation and promised 112 sixth-grade graduates of the Belmont Elementary School a free college education. Through Norman Newberg, a professor at the College of Education, the university became heavily involved in providing programs for these students and resources to the public schools they attended, including University City High. The program succeeded in significantly increasing the number of students who graduated from high school over the norm for the neighborhood, but hopes of catalyzing major educational reforms that would benefit all students were largely dashed. About 10% of the students have gotten 4-year college degrees, again above the norm, one of them from Penn.

The next leap for the Penn–community collaboration is the creation of an entirely new elementary school in the area, from scratch. Part of the motivation is to have a local school where Penn faculty members want to send their children. But the pitfalls will be great, as debates have already erupted over the geographic boundaries of the new school's feeder area— and whether the configuration of its population will drain resources and the most motivated students from the other neighborhood schools.

"There is a lot of conflict embedded in how this new school will be set up," said Shelly Yanoff, director of Philadelphia Citizens for Children and Youth, an advocacy group. "How to make all that work is a challenge." Harkavy said that the partnership will be very involved in making sure it works and doesn't subvert all the assumptions underlying the Penn–neighborhood collaboration in the first place. A Penn-initiated school that ends up excluding significant parts of the neighborhood just won't do, he said.

Penn has been at the center of both a statewide and national network to replicate the work of the partnership. So far, nine universities across the country have adopted the model, including Clark-Atlanta and the University of Alabama at Birmingham. Locally, the Philadelphia Higher Education Network for Neighborhood Development involves 36 institutions and was awarded a grant in 1997 to develop service-learning courses and support community-initiated projects.

"Any university considering such a move must carefully consider its intent," Harkavy said. And several conditions must be in place. University faculty members must see value to their getting involved but not view it as a one-way street which they will gain research knowledge but then abandon the relationship. Universities must be willing to continue the programs after seed money, often provided by grants, has run out. And they must be prepared to reevaluate their very mission in light of the new involvement.

School systems must be flexible enough so that teachers and principals can adapt curricula and schedules to accommodate the new programs. They must be willing to get over what may have been a bad relationship or difficult history with the university in the past. And they have to invest resources in community building and communicating with neighborhood organizations.

In Philadelphia, Harkavy has seen institutional change both in schools and the university, but, he said, it isn't enough. "Penn has done a great deal and could do a great deal more," he said. The mutual benefits are obvious to him and are becoming more obvious to others. "Something related to making things better for most people is the best way to learn," said Harkavy. "It's Dewey's principle of instrumental intelligence. Human beings learn best by confronting real problems in a practical way."

CHAPTER 12

TRINITY HELPS HARTFORD STRUGGLE BACK

Rick Green

Near a street corner surrounded by aging brick apartment buildings, gas stations, and liquor stores, Hector Santiago is shot dead one rainy September afternoon in 1993 in Hartford, Connecticut. As the gunman flees, the victim dies quickly, but the burst of violence is no surprise. Gang fights have been spraying bullets around the Frog Hollow neighborhood for 5 years. This time, though, the killing occurs across the street from Trinity College—its green playing fields, imposing Gothic brownstones, and world of privilege set off from the dismal surroundings by only an 8-foot iron fence.

Students, playing rugby in the afternoon mist, jump the fence and try unsuccessfully to revive Santiago on the bloody corner of Broad Street and Brownell Avenue. Within hours, a citywide curfew seals off the streets and jittery college administrators shut the campus to outsiders. At the college, located in Hartford for almost 175 years, a feeling of panic prevails. Within months, even Tom Gerety, Trinity's idealistic, let's-save-Hartford president, would depart, leaving for, of all places, archrival Amherst College. "It was desperation," Gerety recalled of the mood at the college during the early 1990s. "The neighborhood seemed like hell on wheels."

Now, imagine this same street corner, 6 years later, almost to the exact day and time of Hector Santiago's murder. Rachel Rivera, a graduate of Trinity, stands on the site talking to two boys on bicycles on a warm September evening. Empty buildings still line some streets and the iron fence still divides, but in front of Rivera an entire city block of concrete, iron, and brick is rising. In back of her, the warm glow from the recently opened Boys and Girls Club lights the street. It is an ironic place, Rivera says, "of great dreams," where children who once joined gangs now think of a hopeful future. Dozens come each day, for sports and crafts and homework help at a youth club opened only a few months ago, in the winter of 1999. Meanwhile, Trinity students fan out every day into the neighborhood—on research projects, as mentors, or coaching basketball or soccer games.

What happened during the last half of the 1990s in the neighborhood surrounding Trinity is an unlikely tale of nascent revival in a city perpetually tormented by its long-ago greatness. It is the story of an aggressive plan of attack plotted by Trinity president Evan Dobelle, the unlikely leader of this too-long-cloistered New England liberal arts college. Today, the corner of Broad and Brownell, where Hector Santiago died, is the epicenter of the $200 million Learning Corridor neighborhood-revitalization project. The development, using mostly public money but with a critical $6-million infusion from Trinity, is meant to link the Trinity campus with a major hospital and four innovative new public schools: a public Montessori school, a middle school, a regional science and technology high school program, and a regional performing arts high school. In the process, Trinity is literally unbuttoning itself, spilling forth students and professors into a community once largely shunned and organizing a housing-renewal initiative to bring back the greater Frog Hollow neighborhood.

It is a stunning, if yet unrealized, vision of a community of owner-occupied homes, wired for the twenty-first century, where a child could start out at the neighborhood Montessori school and finish with a degree at Trinity and even the bricklayers for the new schools have been culled from the ranks of the local unemployed.

"This isn't speculative. This isn't a concept. This is real," a confident Dobelle said in 1996, before the block-sized Learning Corridor sprouted from the contaminated dirt in a city lot. This was a bold prediction from the leader of a school that over the years had walled itself off from Hartford and the increasingly impoverished community that surrounded it. If it works, Trinity's aggressive Learning Corridor could become a powerful engine for change that Hartford has long sought—and a savvy survival manual for the endangered liberal arts college. Certainly Trinity is eagerly marketing it as such.

Even more, Dobelle believed he was cutting a pathway for wealthy liberal arts colleges, pushing them to take a look at their neighborhoods as part of their campuses. Small colleges and universities—sometimes the only institutions with healthy bank accounts remaining in these neighborhoods—are uniquely suited to pulling together the different parties vital for a successful urban rebirth, be it in Holyoke, Philadelphia, or Hartford. "We've coasted on our traditions, coasted on our endowments," Dobelle told an audience in a speech at the National Press Club in Washington, D.C., in early 1999. "We are trying to define a new sense of institutional purpose. We must build a community."

Lofty words, but Trinity has emerged as the engineer of the most successful redevelopment project in a city that in 1999 became a national laughingstock during a failed effort to bring the New England Patriots football team to town. While politicians were double-dealing each other over a sports franchise, Dobelle made his unglamorous argument that "intellectual property" can anchor economic growth. Now his project is the one that turns heads—and erects construction cranes. "The engines for change are colleges and universities, because they are there and they cannot deny they are wealthy. Williams has gone over $1 billion in endowment. I'm at $340 million," Dobelle argues. "You are not going to bring manufacturing back into the cities. It is not going to happen," Dobelle says with the confidence that has enabled him to win over local and state politicians to the tune of a public investment of more than $150 million in his project. "You have to make the cities the destination for education, museums, whatever."

The Deteriorating Situation

Hector Santiago's death on the corner of Brownell and Broad that September day in 1993 was another grim chapter in a years-long stretch of gang violence. It came after decades of middle-class flight and the resulting racially segregated schools. Meanwhile, an economic recession ravaged this densely populated neighborhood, squeezing out what was left of a middle-class population. More than half of all residents still live below the poverty line, and another half of adults over 25 haven't completed high school. Few fourth-graders are anywhere close to grade level in reading or writing ability. At one point in the late 1980s, Hartford, a city of 140,000 then, was averaging one drive-by shooting a day. By the early 1990s, state police had been called in to help patrol the streets in the neighborhoods around Trinity, home to Hartford's burgeoning Puerto Rican community and one of the most vibrant Hispanic marketplaces in New England.

For prospective Trinity students, who come largely from privileged suburbia, the deteriorating city surrounding the college was convincing them to go elsewhere. After all, by the time they got off Interstate 84, they and their parents would have to travel past the rows of hollowed-out buildings and street-corner prostitutes before even arriving at Trinity's front gate. The college itself had been growing increasingly anxious for more than two decades, reaching out with small housing-renovation programs neighborhood adult education, as well as setting up a nonprofit partnership with Hartford Hospital, The Institute for Living (a renowned psychiatric hospital), and Connecticut Public Television and Radio, all located nearby.

But by the late 1980s and early 1990s, a feeling of profound worry had taken hold. During one excruciating afternoon, a drive-by shooting occurred in front of a church where the mayor, neighborhood leaders, and top Trinity administrators were meeting. "You would interview kids that came in and you could just feel the nervousness," said Gerety, who deserves more credit than he gets for pushing Trinity to open its gates and renew its commitment to Hartford. "We started seeing Bates [College] beat us in admissions statistics."

"Almost every night some kid from Greenwich's Volvo was getting tampered with," continued Gerety, who arrived at Trinity in 1989, just as gang violence began to peak. He was soon secretly dispatched by jittery trustees to look at possible sites out in bucolic nearby Litchfield County for relocating the college. There, Trinity could retreat back into privileged obscurity, another cookie-cutter version of Williams, Amherst, or Colby. "It was just so tense. I'm telling [the trustees] you have to do something generous and good," he said. "Otherwise how are you going to get these little suburbanites into Hartford with machine guns popping?" Strong-armed police activity, which included imprisoning much of the leadership of violent street gangs and seizing the cars of those patronizing the prostitutes, had quieted the neighborhood down by 1994. But the blight and crushing burden of poverty remained.

Enter Dobelle, who walked in and seemingly took the president's job by acclamation when he floored trustees in his initial interview by presenting a detailed plan for saving Trinity. A former mayor of Pittsfield, Massachusetts, chief of protocol to President Jimmy Carter at age 31, top fund-raiser for the Democratic National Committee, and later community college chancellor in San Francisco, Dobelle was something different: the brashness of Donald Trump combined with an intellectual's profound social conscience. Here was a man with a concrete, if lofty, vision and academic haughtiness. Jewish at what was once a WASP institution, Dobelle was equally comfortable sitting down with a local pastor or a political hack. He was a man who had intimate knowledge of how to turn federal loans and private investment into bricks and mortar. Said Dobelle: "I pretty much knew what I thought needed to be done. I talked to a lot of people and tried to get them to think on a higher level. My vision was a holistic approach to neighborhood revitalization. You had to capture all the elements, from schools to recreation to transportation and housing to retail to spiritual. You had to do it all." Dobelle sounded more like the idealistic mayor he once was than a parsimonious president of a small college in New England. "The failure of urban renewal for 50 years is that they've always gentrified or you clearcut the neighborhood and build it over in your own image, which is what a lot of colleges and institutions do," he said, reprising a speech he has given dozens of times in the last 2 years.

Saving the neighborhood around Trinity was fine and noble, but Dobelle still had to try to solve the same problem that Gerety had struggled with—a declining and lower-achieving pool of applicants. To do that, Trinity had to face a difficult reality: the one great asset that the school had—a culturally rich city neighborhood—was the one that everyone denied.

Getting the Students into the Community

Along with the high-profile bricks and mortar of the 16-acre Learning Corridor site with its campus of four schools, Trinity is pushing students to get out into the community and take advantage of Hartford. The college sees itself as one of the only small liberal arts schools offering students a true urban experience. Applications by 1999 were up more than 50% since the grim days of 1993 and 1994, while at the same time the college had also grown more discriminating, accepting 4 of 10 applicants instead of the 6 of 10 as in the early 1990s. Ninety percent who apply say they're interested in community service. About a quarter of the 2,000 undergraduates are minority.

Rebecca Mayer was the sort of student Trinity had always attracted—a high-achieving teenager from the wealthy Boston suburb of Lexington. In 1999, she was the kind that Trinity is banking on to survive: an earnest 19-year-old who had come to Trinity because of Hartford, not in spite of it. A sophomore, Mayer had spent her first days as a student living in a homeless shelter during Trinity's take on freshman orientation. She worked on a Habitat for Humanity project. This year, she is co-chair of a steering committee that oversees student outreach all over the city. She has worked at the state capitol and with teenagers at the neighborhood Boys and Girls Club, and she has organized a national conference on homelessness and hunger at Trinity.

"A lot of students who come here have never been in a neighborhood like the one Trinity is in," said Mayer. "I am studying how economics can help the development of a community, and that's exactly what the Boys and Girls Club is doing." Still, Mayer said, "a lot of students are scared of this neighborhood. I was scared, but then I went to work at the Boys and Girls Club. There is still so much apathy at Trinity. [Too much] of the campus doesn't do anything. I'm trying to make that change."

One night early in the year, she has gathered with two dozen students at the Boys and Girls Club, which has become the portal for many students to enter the largely impoverished neighborhood of Frog Hollow. In their fleece vests and baseball hats, they sign up to help with homework or sports teams. Among them were Molly Malick, who led an Outward Bound trip over the summer with a group of local high school girls, and Davis Albohm, a sopho-more from Bergen County, New Jersey. "The reason I came to Trinity was because of the city," said Albohm, who rejected the idea of college in a more rural setting. In 1998, he led a group of students from the Hartford Street Youth Project, bringing them on campus every Wednesday.

The school has been encouraging faculty to make the city more a part of their curriculum. Jim Trostle, an associate professor of anthropology, left a professorship with the consortium of five liberal arts colleges around Amherst to come to Trinity in 1998 because of what he heard it was doing in Hart-ford. "I think there are lots of schools experimenting with community-based learning, but on the other hand the depth of the encounter this campus has with the idea is more significant," said Trostle.

"It wasn't just rhetoric. There was money available to redesign courses, money to pay Hartford residents to bring into classes," said Trostle, a former instructor at the National Outdoor Leadership School in Wyoming. Last year, he dispensed with a research paper in one of his classes in favor of a require-ment that students volunteer for at least 20 hours doing research with a com-munity organization, such as transcribing interviews with drug addicts for a medical anthropology class. Academically, Trostle sees community outreach as "helping to create experiences for students that cause them to reflect bet-ter on the reading they are doing in class." In human terms, it's the differ-ence between "driving through the neighborhood quickly because you don't want to get mugged" and taking the time to understand that "those are people living their lives."

To promote the link between college-level research and community needs, the school has also opened its "Trinity Center for Neighborhoods," which operated out of a small building along New Britain Avenue, a street that the school would one day like to see become a vibrant retail cooridor. For now, it remains home to liquor stores, gas stations, and an "Everything for $1" outlet. A "cities data center" was gearing up to collect socioeconomic data on Hartford that professors might one day use. The center also encouraged faculty to do research that community groups can use—such as the relation-ship between crime and truancy or an analysis of where the entry-level jobs around Trinity are.

Neighborhood activist Hyacinth Yennie, president of the group Hart-ford Areas Rally Together, praised Trinity for the effort it has made to reach out, and particularly for supporting construction of the new schools. But she said residents aren't blind to Trinity's motives. "They are bringing in all these rich kids to come to our city, and they want to do everything they can to make the neighborhood better," she said. "But it is important that we the people in the neighborhood are a part of that project. We just don't want to be heard."

Dobelle's Grand Plan

Amid the grand planning and big talk from Dobelle, there were still gaping holes as the 1990s drew to a close. Drive around the Trinity neighborhood and you see the impressive new school buildings that will link the Hartford Hospital campus with Trinity's. But also remaining are the vacant buildings and others in disrepair on every block; there is nothing that resembles a funky college neighborhood—except for a lone restaurant on the edge of the campus that Trinity has been forced to subsidize to keep open. Three years into the project, fewer than a dozen homes had been built or rehabilitated. Part of the problem was the cost: It takes a $180,000 to purchase and renovate a single-family home, while the selling price is capped at $90,000 to make it affordable for low-income families. Major private developers have yet to be attracted, despite the more than $200 million in public and private money being pumped in. The redevelopment project has targeted a 15-square-block area around Trinity, streets lined with aging three-family homes, apartment complexes, and Hartford's own "perfect sixes." These cozy, six-unit brick buildings were erected to house the legions of nineteenth-century immigrants who worked in the factories that made typewriters, bicycles, and guns at a time when Hartford was a wealthy industrial leader.

It was Eddie Perez's job to prowl the streets and put together the deals to revive some of the most distressed areas. Perez, a Trinity vice-president, was on leave in 1999 to work for the alliance of neighborhood institutions that handled the housing revitalization. "I watch every goddamn street," said Perez, a savvy neighborhood insider who grew up in Hartford and was hired by Gerety to act as the college's eyes and ears in the neighborhood. "If you don't make an investment now, you are going to make a bigger investment later," Perez said to a visitor as he drove down a street that he described as having "already tipped in the wrong direction" with abandoned property and vacant buildings. Trinity had moved quickly to finance a Habitat for Humanity redevelopment of an empty building on the street. Trinity and its partners targeted approximately 80 sites for redevelopment either through razing and new construction or rehabilitation. About 30 of the 80 sites have been acquired for development. At least $75 million from Fannie Mae, the Federal National Mortgage Association, has been guaranteed to help renovate and subsidize home ownership for the 15-block area.

Gerety said that two things had not turned around in that neighborhood. Housing continues to deteriorate, according to Gerety, and the private sector does not seem to have a commitment to create jobs for neighborhood residents. "With those two issues they haven't made a dent," said Gerety, who still owns a home in the city.

Ken Greenberg, a Toronto urban planner who helped design Trinity's master plan emphasizing open, public spaces, urges patience. He said that real success requires a substantial commitment over time in order to build up a sense of trust. "The primary targets for the effort are people who already have a stake in the area. But at some point you also start to attract people who are locating to Hartford," Greenberg said.

Although conceding that the housing recovery had not been as dramatic as that of the nonresidential buildings on Broad Street, Perez and Dobelle said that substantial progress was maybe only a year away. Hartford Hospital president John Meehan argued that the intent was not to attract a major employer. Instead, the goal was to create a model for job opportunity. All jobs at the college and at the hospital complex, which includes a children's hospital and the psychiatric Institute for Living, are posted first at a neighborhood job center. The same is true for construction jobs. A neighborhood group, Hartford Areas Rally Together, brought together trade unions and contractors. With a $1-billion downtown redevelopment project on the drawing boards in Hartford, community organizer Yolanda Rivera said that the rest of the city will be looking to the partnership created at Trinity. "I am looking for this project to become the role model for every construction project in this city," said Rivera. "It is bringing people together."

Meehan said the partnership created for the project—between a hospital with a changing mission, a wealthy college, and an impoverished neighborhood—was the real revolution. In the process of pulling the pieces together, all sides realized their common interests. But it took a dramatic raising of the stakes, when gang violence spun out of control, to really push everyone together. "We want adequate housing, safe streets, good schools, jobs. Those are all things that make for a healthy community," said Meehan. "It's for our enlightened self-interest to be involved."

To be sure, the new construction in the neighborhood surrounding Trinity is impressive, but people like Rachel Rivera offer the most hope for the link between Trinity and its neighborhood. The 1999 Trinity graduate arrived from the South Bronx the same time as Dobelle and his fantastic promises. After 4 years of community service, she stayed on in the neighborhood as education director of the newly opened Boys and Girls Club, which by 1999 was serving more than 400 children in a neighborhood that, 12 months before, had nothing of the sort. "Even though Trinity has its own interests, it's good for the community, too. People need to understand that," said Rivera.

Spurred by a rapidly deteriorating neighborhood, Trinity discovered that by aggressively taking the lead—and pumping its human resources and $6 million from its own endowment into the project—a small, wealthy institution can be a powerful redevelopment force. It's an obvious lesson from which other educational institutions could learn, particularly since a college already embedded in a neighborhood is somewhat likely to be viewed with less skepticism than an outside, private developer.

Dobelle's penchant for big ideas did not abate. In early 2000, even as his Learning Corridor neared completion, he announced a $75-million redevelopment plan for the other side of campus—away from the Learning Corridor project—in a crumbling neighborhood known as "Behind the Rocks." This time, using connections he made years earlier while mayor of Pittsfield, Massachusetts, Dobelle said that he lined up world-famous architect Frank O. Gehry to design a 115,000–square-foot Connecticut History Center. It was to become home to the state's historical society. Gehry won acclaim for the Guggenheim Museum he designed in Bilbao, Spain, which was called one of the great buildings of the twentieth century when it opened in 1997. Although money would have to be raised for the historical society project, few doubted that Dobelle's commitment to making things work would work again in Hartford.

Still, the success of the Trinity project hinges significantly on an unusual leader. In this case it is a college president willing to spend long hours in church basements and hospital board rooms and in cultivating neighborhood politicians, in addition to doing the usual fund-raising college presidents must engage in. Dobelle's trick was not to look for special help, but rather to take advantage of the myriad existing sources of revenue, weaving together school construction grants, federal housing dollars, foundation grants, and other sources into one redevelopment project.

On a cold November afternoon in 1999, not 4 years after Dobelle's arrival, a presidential motorcade barreled through the streets surrounding Trinity, stopping at a busy Hispanic marketplace. For Trinity officials and the Frog Hollow neighborhood, President Bill Clinton's visit, part of a national tour to highlight urban reinvestment, was further evidence of new life in a neighborhood near death a few years earlier. Along Brownell Avenue, a short one-block street, three-family homes are finally selling. An apartment building has been renovated. A new post office has opened a block away. Even the Girl Scouts will soon arrive, setting up a regional headquarters one street away. A neighborhood computer center and preschool, plus another "center for families," will also soon open.

By the fall of 2000, the centerpiece—a Learning Corridor of four innovative new public schools—is scheduled to open, a place where 1,500 children from preschool through twelfth grade from the neighborhood and region would come to a neighborhood once feared, even by those living there. "Here you can make a difference," Rivera said, explaining why she chose Hartford over going elsewhere. "In New York, 400 children is nothing. Here, it is a huge impact. Kids, kids are the bridge."

WHAT HAVE WE LEARNED?

The case studies collected here are snapshots of efforts to strengthen the often-tenuous relationships between the public schools and colleges and universities. Each case has a lesson for all who believe that the gap between these two sectors must be narrowed if education is, indeed, to become the seamless process to which so many give lip service. The gap is neither new nor benign. It is a corrosive force, undermining state and national imperatives for improving education and for meeting the needs of more students. This concluding chapter identifies public policy issues and the directions that should be pursued to initiate and support promising collaborative programs.

This book is organized around five substantive policy issues—governance, equity, standards, teachers, and community buildings—each of which is highly complex and controversial in its own right. Each area is examined in the specific context of collaboration. How did these issues arise in the 12 collaborative programs that, explicitly or implicitly, aim to strengthen cooperation between the colleges and the public schools?

Governance

Good educational governance can improve student outcomes. Presumably, to take this theory to the next step, if the two sectors were to build cooperative structures, it would be easier to achieve educational objectives. Yet it remains to be demonstrated in a definitive way that this assumption is correct or that models can be found for carrying out effective collaboration in governance. Programs in Massachusetts and Colorado illustrate what has been tried.

Massachusetts

In 1989, Boston University and its then-president, John L. Silber, accepted an invitation from the Chelsea School Committee to manage its failing school system. The result: Boston University has been firmly in charge of day-today operations of the Chelsea schools for the past 10 years. The School Committee retained oversight, could overrule the university's management, and, indeed, could terminate the agreement.

University faculty members—some with specific grants—from many disciplines volunteered to work with the Chelsea schools, and Chelsea teachers became team leaders in the program. Over the past decade, test scores and attendance have increased, but not dramatically. The major improvement, however, is real but almost impossible to quantify: Chelsea schools are no longer simply custodial, but are becoming institutions for learning. Silber, described as "cocksure" and "iconoclastic," is clearly responsible for the success of the program. The School Committee and Boston University have agreed to continue their partnership until 2002–2003. Whether the old lethargy and the era of corruption will return with Boston University's departure remains to be seen.

Colorado

A different approach to collaboration in governance was established in Colorado in 1990 by the Educational Alliance of Pueblo. The Alliance brought together the University of Southern Colorado and Pueblo School District 60 to raise the performance of the schools and to cut costs by combining business services. Its most innovative characteristic was the initial appointment of the district superintendent as a vice-president of the university.

The Alliance has had some success in bringing district teachers and university faculty members together, mainly in science and mathematics. Anecdotal evidence suggests that schools have improved. But critics believe that the Alliance exists mainly on paper. Measures of success are hard to find; criteria for evaluation have not been established. The hope that structural change at the top administrative levels would filter down to encourage creative collaboration has been largely unrealized. Turnover at the top leadership levels has reduced the program's initial momentum; the university has had three presidents, and the school district four superintendents, since 1990.

BOTH OF THESE CASE STUDIES concern governance. In the Boston University program, structural change was accompanied by commensurate changes in real authority spearheaded by an unusually charismatic college leader. In Pueblo, structural change did not coexist with real changes in authority. It is not clear that either program could or should be replicated or transferred elsewhere. Each cautions us, however, that desires to improve education by streamlining governing arrangements are matched by problems that formal structures can present. Continuity of leadership, for instance, is not assured by a formal institutional title. And governing structures imposed unilaterally from the top may alienate participants unprepared for abrupt organizational change. It remains to be seen how much effect collaborative governance can have on education.

Equity

Equal opportunity is the basic American value that pervades all the case studies. Education beyond high school has become almost the only key that will open the door to a better life, socially and economically, for most citizens. All Americans deserve an education that will enable them to work at a living wage and—if qualified and motivated—to attend college, regardless of their financial resources, ethnic background, or geographic location. Programs to achieve equity generally fall into one of two categories: *school-centered* programs that focus on an entire school and *student-centered* programs that focus on particular groups of students. Three programs are particularly relevant to equity, those in California, Tennessee, and Texas.

California

The University of California and California State University—the state's two senior higher education systems—are sprawling, separately governed organizations. Campuses of both systems have traditionally operated outreach programs to increase college opportunity. The number and variety of these programs bloomed in the 1990s, when racial or ethnic criteria could no longer be used to select applicants for admission. In part, these new efforts were built on a belief in the benefits of a diverse student body. In larger part, perhaps the two systems recognized the need for continuing public and governmental goodwill in a state where Latinos and African Americans now comprise a majority of the schoolchildren. Hundreds of programs are now under way, but neither the state nor the systems have an overall plan for increasing minority enrollment.

A leading example of a school-centered program is the Long Beach Education Partnership, a collaboration of California State University, Long Beach, the local community college, and the school district. The goal was "seamless education" from kindergarten through college. The Partnership successfully created a context in which university faculty and public school teachers worked together toward shared goals, the schools adopted rigorous standards, and high school exit exams are soon expected to be aligned with the university's entrance exams. Richard Riley, U.S. Secretary of Education, called the program "a wonderful example of all of the parts of American education fitting together." The University of California at Los Angeles provides an example of a student-centered program in its Career-Based Outreach Program, which hires students to tutor some 80 ninth-, tenth-, and eleventh-graders at 19 low-performing high schools. The aim was to make these students competitive with students from any other school.

Tennessee

Middle College High School in Memphis, located on the campus of Shelby State Community College, has as its goal reaching underachieving students believed to have college potential and guiding them into higher education. Although it comprises a single school, the program is essentially student-centered, concentrating on at-risk students. At Middle College High, students have visible peer models in the college students, receive superior academic and support services, and are encouraged to earn simultaneous high school and college credit. Test scores have risen and student attrition has fallen in comparison with other district schools. High school teachers are encouraged to teach in the college, and college faculty help the teachers. A current plan would enlist college faculty to create a curriculum that would close the gap between the last year of high school and the first year of college. For Shelby State, establishing Middle College High was entirely an administrative decision. Faculty members were given little or no notice of it, their complaints were legion, and they called it "Hoodlum High." The school principal was patient, and, eventually, a new college president gave strong support to the school.

Texas

The El Paso Collaborative had its origin in teacher and administrative dissatisfaction with the quality of instruction in the schools in a county where 42% of the children live below the federal poverty level. An offer to help came from the El Paso campus of the University of Texas. The Collaborative's original thrust was to establish a standards-based curriculum based on state-mandated tests of reading, writing, and mathematics. Each school could adapt its own form of the standards-based curriculum. The focus on the curriculum carried over to restructuring professional development and teacher preparation, to building the leadership capacity of principals and other school administrators, and to engaging parents and community leaders in supporting and shaping the reform efforts.

Initial reluctance by some teachers and faculty has been largely overcome, and the program has survived several changes of district leadership. Both this continuity and the comprehensive scope of the program may well be attributed in part to the Collaborative's high-level, representative board. Success may also have been facilitated by El Paso's self-contained character: The university draws 85% of its students from El Paso County and prepares about 80% of the teachers in the county's schools.

These studies reveal the wide variety of collaborative programs that could serve to enhance educational equity. Some, such as the school-centered El Paso Collaborative, may be helped by their identity with a geographic locale. The student-centered Memphis Middle College High suggests that sometimes a new institution in a new location may be an effective way to accomplish change. Both school-centered and student-centered programs are found in California, but the efforts seem to be largely fragmented pilot projects. A major policy question remains: How can such discrete programs within and across California and the nation be assessed, funded, and, where appropriate, coordinated for both economy and long-term effectiveness?

Standards

Standards-based reform programs are almost infinite in their variety. Most share four characteristics: (1) a framework that sets out what students should know and be able to do at a particular grade level; (2) curricula intended to convey this; (3) assessment tools to measure student achievement in terms of the framework; and (4) rewards or penalties for districts, schools, or students for meeting the standards or failing to do so.[1] Our interest focuses on three attempts—in Maryland, Oregon, and Georgia—to align standards for high school graduation with those for college admission.

Maryland

The Partnership for Teaching and Learning, K–16 began in 1995, and continues as an informal triumvirate of three top officials: the chancellor of the University of Maryland system, the state superintendent of public instruction, and the secretary of Maryland's Higher Education Commission, a gubernatorial appointee. The Partnership's three objectives are higher academic standards, reform of teacher education, and equal opportunity. The Business Roundtable has joined the effort. Equal opportunity may be the most difficult of the three objectives. A chemist at a historically Black college that is a major educator of teachers says, "The toughest issue is equity. . . . If you make the argument that we need to raise standards, then everyone should be on a level playing field. Unfortunately, they're not."

Nevertheless, the K–16 Partnership has had some success: (1) High school graduation and minimum university admission requirements—although not content- or performance-focused—have been aligned. (2) A 2-year effort produced faculty and teacher agreement on the elements of an essay that would receive a passing grade. (3) Professional development schools are proliferating. An experienced outside observer believes that the Partnership has been "remarkably successful."[2] The major concern is the Partnership's continuing reliance on the three founding leaders. If one or two leave office, the Partnership might be vulnerable.

Oregon

In Oregon, the catalyst for collaboration was a 1991 law that called for setting performance standards and creating two new credentials, one for the first 2 years of high school, and one for the final 2. Boards of education and higher education institutions met jointly to discuss improving cooperation, and their outcome was to create the Proficiency-Based Admissions Standards System (PASS). Through PASS, higher education would list the skills and knowledge expected of freshmen and would work with the schools to determine the proficiencies required for the two new credentials.

The Oregon PASS program centers on the development of new performance standards intended to connect high school instruction to college admission requirements. Although PASS is still a work in progress, students in the pilot programs talk of the new credentials and admission standards as the same thing. No state has moved deeper into proficiency-based admissions than Oregon. It is not yet clear, however, whether this national reputation is valued in Oregon. The Oregon Board of Higher Education rarely discusses PASS, the state Department of Education is described as "a reluctant partner," and state leaders have not issued policy guidelines to promote it. Teachers are concerned about being buried in paperwork as samples of proficiency proliferate. Indeed, many educators and most parents and students remain totally in the dark about these standards.

Georgia

In 1997, Georgia launched its P–16 Initiative, a collaboration similar to that in Maryland. The Initiative includes the 34 campuses of the University System of Georgia, the K–12 Department of Education, local school boards, the state's technical schools and teacher accreditation agency, and representatives of business. Concerned about unprepared applicants and responding to criticism that the colleges were ignoring the public schools, the University System was, and continues to be, the moving force behind the Initiative.

Unlike Maryland with its single, statewide K–16 Partnership, Georgia created 15 regional P–16 councils to operate under the guidelines of the 40-

member statewide Georgia P–16 Council. The state and regional councils can only recommend actions, but the programs they sponsor are considered successful, even at this early date. A later governor appointed the Education Reform Study Commission to put more muscle into the collaborative effort. Furthermore, the Performance Assessment for College and Technical School (PACTS) program is a pilot program, the ultimate aim of which is statewide performance standards for college admissions.

A MAJOR POLICY ISSUE raised by the Maryland, Oregon, and Georgia cases concerns the ability to sustain long-term, high-level political interest. Contrast, for example, the strong statewide leadership in Maryland and Georgia with the apparently weakening support in Oregon. We wonder whether educational standards are a sufficiently compelling issue for policy leaders to see the programs through to completion.

Teachers

The quality of teaching, a major public policy issue for elementary and secondary schools, has now become a key issue in many schools of education as well. A school of education trains teachers and sends them out as instructors of pupils in the public schools; these pupils eventually enroll in the university. Then, all too often, college faculty members complain that these students are ill prepared for college-level work. The loop is not difficult to discern. The two case studies discuss programs in Ohio and Mississippi.

Ohio

The University of Cincinnati is regarded as a national leader in connecting teacher training to the public schools. The program originated with the school district and the teachers' union and was immediately embraced by the university. Theory and practice are linked through cooperation between the university and the district as aspiring teachers—90 in 1999—spend a fifth year at the university working as paid interns in one of nine participating city schools. Staff at each school vote on whether to participate in the program. The major success of the program is measured by student satisfaction: Attrition in the teacher-training program is down, and the number of graduates taking teaching positions is up.

Moreover, the program is said to have developed student interest in, and loyalty to, instruction of inner-city school children among those preparing to teach. Fiscal support for the program is problematic, however, depending on unstable district funding, and schools have shown a reluctance to volunteer to participate. Nor has the program resulted in any substantial connections or collaborations between university faculty members and schoolteachers. A major problem is continuity of leadership, since the initial founders have departed.

Mississippi

Jackson State University's Institute for Educational Renewal has three programs to improve teacher education: (1) assisting master teachers in attaining certification by the National Board for Professional Teaching Standards, (2) providing in-service education for veteran teachers, and (3) delivering advanced training for Head Start personnel. Its programs show, on one hand, the benefits of state and federal funding and initiatives, and, on the other, the problems that can arise from apparent lack of strong state leadership.

The Institute's master teacher program responds to a state initiative that provides $2,000 reimbursement to candidates for National Board certification, and, if certification is achieved, an annual pay raise for 10 years, the life of the certificate. The National Board has recognized the Mississippi initiative as a model for other states. The program for veteran teachers takes faculty to rural schools to bring instruction—for example, computer training—to those for whom attendance at the campus would be a hardship. These outreach programs are largely designed at the school level. Participation by the teachers is, however, problematic. The U.S. Department of Health and Human Services supports the Institute's Head Start program, which is intended to reach rural areas, a goal that has made it difficult to attract regular university faculty. All three programs of the Institute are less than 5 years old, and none has been evaluated.

THE PROGRAMS IN Ohio and Mississippi are quite different. The Ohio initiative highlights the critical importance of collaboration for encouraging aspiring teachers to devote themselves to working in the public schools, though support has waxed and waned. The Mississippi program appears to have accomplished its goal of reaching rural teachers and administrators, but it could, we suggest, have achieved greater results with more committed state and institutional guidance and support than it apparently has received this far.

Community Building

We use "community" to describe a neighborhood in which the people who share a geographic niche also have common concerns about improving life in that setting. Community building may, as in the case of the El Paso Collaborative, be a by-product of local efforts specifically addressed to educational issues. In contrast, creation of a more livable neighborhood that reinforces the school in its midst was the impetus for collaborative relationships in Pennsylvania and Connecticut.

Pennsylvania

The Center for Community Partnerships at the University of Pennsylvania traces its origin to the 1985 police bombing to dislodge the MOVE group from a row house, killing 11 people and burning two city blocks. The Center is a mature program that started with a small grant for a modest summer program but that expanded rapidly when large-scale city funding became available. After 15 years, the program offers 96 field-oriented courses in nearly all of the university's 12 schools and colleges. Under the direction of a faculty member and a local schoolteacher–coordinator, students from Penn work and do research at neighborhood elementary and secondary schools. Parents and others in the community participate in such programs as those involving nutrition and oral history. The collaboration has survived despite wavering interest as school principals changed over the years. Nine universities across the country have adopted the model.

Connecticut

A murder across the street from Trinity College capped a history of petty theft and vandalism, convincing Trinity leadership that they either had to move the college or improve the neighborhood. Trinity's Learning Corridor project will link the campus with a major hospital and four new and innovative public schools. Neighborhood children and Trinity students now gather at a recently opened youth center—actually at the corner where the murder occurred—for sports, crafts, and homework help. Trinity students fan out into the neighborhood on research projects as mentors and coaches. Faculty are encouraged to make the city a part of the curriculum. Trinity had, of course, its own interest in creating a livable neighborhood. By enhancing the viability of the surrounding neighborhood, Trinity has made itself a more attractive institution to potential students.

MOST COLLEGES STRIVE for better town–gown relationships, but at what point does this and should this become community building? In Pennsylvania and Connecticut, violent incidents impelled urgently needed closer contact with the community, and the results are rewarding. But should essentially unilateral community building in the sense of real estate development and gentrification generally be a major objective of college and public school collaboration? Or, absent the particular circumstances of the University of Pennsylvania and Trinity College, is not community building in the sense of shared values and goals both the means and the end of *educational* collaborations—as seems to be the case of the El Paso Collaborative?

Final Words

What do these 12 studies have in common? Great complexity is surely a thread that runs through all. An evaluator of Cincinnati's successful program observes that collaboration "requires institutional changes in districts, in schools, in classrooms, in higher education administration, in higher education faculty, and in unions. That's pretty much the whole universe."[3] Collaboration may also require changes in public policy. Changing "a whole universe" may be possible, but it cannot be done without dedicated proponents, hard work, adequate funding, and patience for long-term results.

For all of their strengths, weaknesses, and uncertainties, each of the 12 approaches raises important policy questions that we can only begin to explore. We have found no formula for effective collaboration, but there are lessons and caveats that transcend and cut across the cases. We believe that the five categories into which these case studies are organized provide a useful framework for exploring collaborative programs and strategies.

But the 12 cases are among a relatively small number of pioneering efforts that seek to fill a significant vacuum in American education. They represent, even with their shortcomings, the exceptions, not the rule, when it comes to collaboration. Most states and communities lack an institutional forum for even beginning a conversation about both schools and colleges, much less for initiating substantive collaboration. In the absence of incentives and accountability, collaboration is destined to remain reliant on episodic leadership initiatives, altruism, and volunteerism. The two worlds of education are destined to remain different until public policy and public finance operate in tandem. The work toward making that happen has only begun.

Notes

1. See Deborah Meier, "Educating a Democracy," the introductory essay to the topic, "Do We Need Educational Standards?" in the *Boston Review*'s New Democracy Forum (Dec. 1999/Jan. 2000). Eight other essays debate the pros and cons of standards.

2. Kati Haycock, president, Education Trust.

3. See Chapter 9.

Questions to Consider

Illustrations of questions explored by chapter contributors:

1. What was the genesis of the program or initiative?
   Who were the prime movers and what were their motivations?
   Was this a replication of some other program, somewhere else?
2. What facilitated the program's development?
3. What were the deterrents?
4. What are the prospects for sustaining the program?
5. In what ways has the program been successful and/or unsuccessful?
   What are the concrete indicators of success/lack of success?
6. What are the continuing obstacles?
7. As far as the higher education side is concerned . . .
   What have been the positives and negatives?
   What has been the extent of faculty participation?
   In what ways have parts of the institution beyond the college of education been involved in the program?
8. As far as the elementary/secondary side is concerned . . .
   What have been the positives and the negatives?
   What has been the extent of participation?
   What has been the role of the principal, the school district?
9. What lessons have been learned that might be useful in other attempts at collaboration?
   What do policy makers and educators have to bear in mind as a result of the experience of this program?
10. What have been the attempts at replication?

ABOUT THE EDITORS AND THE CONTRIBUTORS

Gene I. Maeroff is the director of the Hechinger Institute on Education and the Media at Teachers College, Columbia University. He was formerly a senior fellow with the Carnegie Foundation for the Advancement of Teaching and, before that, national education correspondent of the *New York Times*. His most recent book is *Altered Destinies: Making Life Better for Schoolchildren in Need*.

Patrick M. Callan is president of the National Center for Public Policy and Higher Education. He has served as executive director of the California Higher Education Policy Center, the California Postsecondary Education Commission, the Washington State Council for Postsecondary Education, and the Montana Commission on Postsecondary Education. He has written extensively about educational policy.

Michael D. Usdan has been president since 1981 of the Institute for Educational Leadership, a Washington, D.C.–based hands-on think tank with diverse policy and leadership development programs in more than 40 states. He was formerly Connecticut's Commissioner of Higher Education and president of the Merrill-Palmer Institute in Detroit. He also has been a public school teacher and university professor, as well as having served as a member and as president of the school board in New Rochelle, New York.

Mickie Anderson is a K–12 education reporter for the *Commercial Appeal* in Memphis. The Florida native has also covered education and law enforcement at the *Orlando Sentinel* and the *Tampa Tribune*. She lives with her husband, pet greyhound, and cat.

Janet Bingham has been an education writer at the *Denver Post* since 1984, covering kindergarten through twelfth grade.

Sam Bingham has been a teacher and curriculum writer and is now a freelance writer based in Denver.

Mike Bowler is the education editor of the *Baltimore Sun*. He has been a reporter, editorial writer, and op-ed editor for the *Sun* during his 30 years at the newspaper and is a former president of the Education Writers Association.

Dave Curtin has been the higher education reporter at the *Denver Post* since 1997.

Duchesne Paul Drew is an education reporter for the *Star Tribune* in Minneapolis. He has written extensively about a number of education topics, including school desegregation, testing, and early childhood education. A native New Yorker, he became familiar with Texas's accountability movement while covering education for the *Dallas Morning News*.

Monique Fields, a graduate of Auburn University at Montgomery, began her career in 1992 at *The Montgomery Advertiser* in Montgomery, Alabama. In 1997, she received a master's degree in journalism from Northwestern University in Evanston, Illinois, and joined *The Tennessean* in Nashville as a higher education reporter. She now writes for the *St. Petersburg Times*.

William Graves has been covering education for 14 years, the last 10 at *The Oregonian* in Portland, Oregon. He is immediate past president of the Education Writers Association and co-author of a book on education reform, *Poisoned Apple*.

Rick Green covers education at the *Hartford Courant*, where he has been a staff writer since 1987. He is a graduate of Northwestern University and has won numerous national awards for his work. He lives in West Hartford with his wife and three children.

Lonnie Harp was the state education reporter for the *Courier-Journal* in Louisville, Kentucky. He has extensively covered student testing issues and teacher quality initiatives connected to the 1990 Kentucky Education Reform Act. He worked for 7 years as a reporter and editor at *Education Week* in Washington, D.C.

Dale Mezzacappa has been covering education for the *Philadelphia Inquirer* since 1986. A journalist for 28 years, she worked at *The Record* in Hackensack, New Jersey, before joining the *Inquirer* in 1979. Prior to taking the education beat, she covered government and politics and was a Nieman Fellow at Harvard University in 1990–1991.

Lee D. Mitgang has reported and written about education, business, urban affairs, communications technologies, and architecture. Following 20 years at the Associated Press and United Press International, he was a senior fellow of the Carnegie Foundation for the Advancement of Teaching. He is now communication director of Wallace-Reader's Digest Funds and a contributing editor of *Architectural Record*. His latest book is *Big Bird and Beyond*.

Ernie Suggs is on the staff of the *Journal and Constitution* in Atlanta, where he has covered education.

Kenneth R. Weiss is an education writer at the *Los Angeles Times*, focusing primarily on trends in higher education in California and throughout the country. He has been on staff at the *Times*, as both a reporter and editor, for more than a decade. He is a graduate of the University of California, Berkeley.